"Why Didn't She Keep Me?"

"Why Didn't She Keep Me?"

Answers to the question every adopted child asks...

by BARBARA BURLINGHAM-BROWN

Langford Books
South Bend, Indiana
1994

"Why Didn't She Keep Me?"

10 9 8 7 6 5 4 3 2

Manufactured in the United States of America

Langford Books,
an imprint of
Diamond Communications, Inc.
Post Office Box 88
South Bend, Indiana 46624-0088
(219) 299-9278
FAX (219) 299-9296

Library of Congress Cataloging-in-Publication Data

Burlingham-Brown, Barbara.
"Why didn't she keep me?" : answers to the question every adopted child asks-- / Barbara Burlingham-Brown.
p. cm.
ISBN 0-912083-66-2
1. Birthmothers--United States--Interviews. 2. Unmarried mothers--United States--Interviews. 3. Adoption--United States. I. Title.
HV875.55.B87 1993
362.83'92'0973--dc20 93-29241
CIP

Contents

Foreword vii

Acknowledgments ix

Introduction xi

ANONYMOUS xiii

1. GENEVIEVE 1
2. PAULA 11
3. CONNIE 17
4. SARAH 29
5. BECKY 40
6. LISA 48
7. K.J. 58
8. TAMI 62
9. CATHLEEN 64
10. KRISTEN 72
11. CHRIS 81
12. DONNA 90
13. ELIZABETH 102
14. MARY KAY 107
15. KIM 118
16. CLAIRE 128
17. LESLIE 136
18. BRIGITTE 145
19. HILARY 153
20. BETH 159

FOREWORD

"Why Didn't She Keep Me?" presents invaluable insight into the life experiences of women who have placed their children for adoption. Through the listening and recording of a competent social worker, Barbara Burlingham-Brown, a comprehensive picture of the adoption experience is captured. With a richness related through a wide variety of cases that span 60 years, this book generates an increased sensitivity and compassion for birthmothers.

As readers take glimpses into the minds and hearts of birthmothers, they see that every adoption experience is unique. Some accounts stir every emotion, as compelling and heartwrenching portraits are drawn. Other narratives elicit an intellectual response as birthmothers describe their experiences more matter-of-factly. *"Why Didn't She Keep Me?"* continually beckons the reader onward, as each version unveils still another significant facet of the adoption process.

The book teaches that relinquishment is never made lightly, that mothers place their children out of love, and that being part of the creation process changes a woman forever. We hear themes of loneliness, rejection, shame, and also those of contentment, fulfillment and satisfaction. We learn that adoption is not only a legal transaction but also a lifelong process. Adoption never concludes in a day or two because no magical line of demarcation exists where this is the past and that is the future. Birthmothers attest to the fact that relinquishment is never forgotten; some pain always remains. Separation, forever difficult, tests the limits of even the strongest of women.

This compilation of birth stories describes a history of adoption in the United States as it has unfolded over the last half of the 20th century. As it becomes clear that the secrecy of traditional adoption harms more than helps people, the many advantages of totally open adoption become apparent.

Birth and adoptive parents establish and maintain supportive rather than adversarial relationships in open adoption. Women from the most deprived and abusive backgrounds can still find meaning and peace through open adoption, perhaps because they take an active role as they pursue options for their children. Conversely, what is often striking about the stories of closed adoption is that women are frequently told what to do by people who think they know best. Often these well-intentioned family members, friends and professionals have not listened to the birthmother's story and therefore lack empathy and a real understanding of adoption from her vantage point.

The presentation of many different types of adoptions—agency, private, closed, semi-open and open adoption—defines the complexity of the adoption process. Any person who desires a fuller understanding of the adoption experience—birthparents, adoptees, adoptive parents, social workers, nurses, attorneys, doctors, judges—will benefit from a reading of this work. It may be especially helpful for adoptees in search and for adoptive parents who want to turn the love they have always felt for their child's birthmother into visible, concrete action.

"Why Didn't She Keep Me?" provides an opportunity for the birthmother's viewpoint to be told and retold. This is paramount, for it is the birthmother who gives the most precious offering—life. We must carefully listen in order to fully appreciate why her gift has no parallel in the human experience.

Dr. Elizabeth L. Rompf

Dr. Elizabeth Rompf is a Certified Open Adoption Counselor and teaches in the College of Social Work at the University of Kentucky. She has research and written extensively on the subject of adoption, open adoption in particular, and regularly conducts workshops and lectures on the topic. Dr. Rompf is also a member of the board of the National Federation for Open Adoption Education.

Acknowledgments

These first-person accounts of the birthmother experience would not have been possible without the willingness of each woman I interviewed to share intimate details of an acutely stressful period of her life. Though most birthmothers did not object to identifying themselves, pseudonyms were used for all first names to protect their privacy as well as that of extended family, birthfathers, adoptive families, etc... I feel privileged to be a witness to their courage and wish them peace in living with the consequences of their adoption decision.

My appreciation also goes to the many adoptive parents and adult adoptees who were pleased at the prospect of this project; to Dr. Elizabeth Rompf who was part of my introduction and commitment to open adoption philosophy in 1991; to the publisher, Jill Langford, for making a commitment to the often neglected member of the adoption triad—the birthmother; and to my husband, Robert C. Brown who patiently—and always with good humor—transcribed hundreds of pages of material!

Introduction

The motivation for this collection of "stories" told in the words of women who placed their children for adoption came from two sources—professional and personal. In 1969 my husband, Clif Burlingham, told me he had been adopted by his parents (who were already deceased). At first I accepted that fact simply as a curious bit of information, but before long I learned how haunted Clif was by not knowing the answers to the questions of his origin.

In his late teens, Clif began searching for his birthparents. Though he learned that they were a married couple, probably in financial distress, their last name as well as his birthmother's maiden name and city of birth, he was not successful in locating them. Wanting some sort of connection, he assumed his birth name as his identity and it was that name he carried to his death in 1984.

On a professional level, I have worked with hundreds of women of all ages and backgrounds who seriously considered voluntarily placing their children in another family. Many of them ask for written material relating the experiences of other women who chose adoption. While there are a few individual stories, I could not find one book that offered in some depth examples of a variety of situations. Thus I placed an ad in newspapers and attended several "search" groups, making contact with dozens of women who were then interviewed for this book.

My selection of the "stories" presented was based on each containing a different set of circumstances leading to an adoption choice. The word "choice" is used even though most of the women who signed releases of their parental rights in the 1960s-70s did not feel they truly had other options. Certainly, they did not have the opportunity to receive the amount of information concerning the adoptive families or the welfare of their birthchildren through the years after placement as women today generally do.

An important part of the adoption process is education, helping infertile couples who want so much to be parents understand why someone who carries a child to term does not exercise the parental right. It seems to me that while most adoptive couples can identify intellectually with the reasons a woman chooses adoption—for example: a poor economic situation, wanting two parents, wanting to pursue educational goals—that the majority are reluctant to recognize on a very real level—or very long—that their joy at becoming parents is contingent on someone else's pain. Most adoption professionals, I think, have heard some version of, "We've had the baby for a year now. What do you mean *she* would like another photograph? Hasn't she gotten on with her life?"

The more aware a family is of what a birthmother experiences, the more likely they are to be empathic with her need to know what has happened to her birthchild beyond the hospital room. While I do not in any way mean to lessen the role of the involved birthfather, my focus for this book has been the birthmother. It is indeed *her role, her decision* that an adoptee questions first.

James Baldwin in *The Evidence of Things Not Seen* (pp. xii) captures the essence and the urgency that lies behind that question: *"I do not remember, will never remember how I howled and screamed the first time...what one does not remember dictates actually, whether one plays poker, pool or chess. What one does not remember contains the key to one's tantrums or one's poise...what one does not remember dictates who one loves or fails to love..."*

—Barbara Burlingham-Brown

Anonymous

For several weeks her family noticed that she seemed to be gaining weight. The long flannel shirts she wore bulged suspiciously but she didn't say anything about having a boyfriend and she was over 21, certainly old enough to be responsible for herself. Confronted, she denied that she was pregnant—it was, she remarked, probably the result of too much overindulgence.

There were other matters for the family to deal with. It was not mentioned again. She went to work each day, and although she became more quiet than usual, generally, she seemed to be her normal self. One hot, summer evening the family gathered to play cards, choosing the screened porch for some relief from the heat. The game went on well past midnight at which time she excused herself, needing to visit the bathroom.

Her mother, father, brother and sisters waited, using the break to munch popcorn, refresh their drinks and remark on the sounds of insects in the night. When she returned, she apologized for the delay, her stomach was upset, probably the result of the heat. It was another hour before a sister also left the room for the bathroom, her screams bringing an end to the card game.

"I don't know anything about a baby," she told the paramedics. "I didn't know I was pregnant," she told the nurse at the hospital. "I never missed a period," she told the doctor. Calmly, evenly, without emotion, she repeated her denials. There was blood all over that bathroom floor, she knew nothing about its source. There was a baby girl, head first in the toilet, she could not imagine where she came from. She only remembered the card game, a pleasant evening with her family.

The doctor spoke with her mother. The baby was full

term, over 8 lbs., perfectly formed though she had never drawn a breath of air. Briefly, crying, her mother held the dead infant and named her Marie. A doll's dress was purchased for burial and a plot was chosen in a rural cemetery, quite a distance from the family home. She said nothing as her mother made these arrangements.

Without ceremony, the infant was buried and grass quickly covered the area, marked only by a cemetery stake. Within the family, no one spoke of the matter again.

Following are the stories told by 20 women or young girls who also experienced an unexpected, unplanned pregnancy, who discovered within themselves the ability to assess their situation and make difficult decisions for themselves and for their babies. For whatever reason, Marie's mother was unable to face the reality that she was carrying a baby, unable to accept the responsibility for her child's life or her death. These narratives may contain a clue to her behavior. They also provide the opportunity to remember a tiny child.

This book is dedicated to Marie, who was born and died in August 1978, a child who had no welcome in the world to which she was born.

GENEVIEVE

"Thirty years ago, things were so much different than today. My daughter was bound to be called a bastard and that was not what I envisioned for her."

In 1985, 25 years after the birth of her daughter, Genevieve contacted the agency through which the adoption took place to provide updated medical information that she felt was important. Genevieve had been treated for cervical cancer at age 29; now at 46, she was completely well, happily married and the mother of two almost-grown sons. She also wanted to know about the well-being of her birthdaughter, whom she named Meghan.

Surprised to hear that Meghan's first name was—by coincidence—the same name given to her by her adoptive parents, Genevieve was unhappy to discover that her birthdaughter was suffering from a chronic disease that usually resulted in early death. Anxious and torn between wanting to communicate with Meghan, yet not wanting to intrude on her family, Genevieve waited for further contact. After three years, she again contacted the adoption agency. This time she was afraid that Meghan's health could have deteriorated and that she would not even be aware of her death.

Fortunately, Meghan at age 28 was managing her physical condition very well, was a graduate student and somewhat ambivalent about her feelings towards contact of any sort with her birthmother. Neither Meghan nor her parents could understand why Genevieve had not known long before of Meghan's condition. Having been told it was genetic, they had informed the agency when Meghan was diagnosed at the age of two that her birthmother was "a carrier" of the disease.

Genevieve wrote a letter to Meghan, including the poem she had written two weeks after her birth. At Christmas 1992 Meghan responded with a letter and photos. Genevieve remarked, "She's been a part of me all these years..."

"WHY DIDN'T SHE KEEP ME?"

Meghan - 1964

Forever in my heart will live the memory
of the tiny angel God sent to me.
I know that today and beyond tomorrow
it will be my cross, my everlasting sorrow.
I'll never hear her laugh or watch her play,
the baby girl I gave away.

From the moment of conception, a woman is a mother, that's my feeling and that's why I am against abortion. From that moment, a woman has to do what's best for the child. Looking back after almost 30 years I can say I would still recommend adoption, especially if the girl, the mother, is in a situation where she is young, uneducated and in no position to care for herself, much less a child. Yes, I miss my daughter and though I have two sons, I've never had another daughter. I don't know that I will ever have contact with her, that is something I have to live with—hoping she will some day decide to respond to me.

As a child, I was spoiled terribly. I had two older brothers and my family lived in the country. My father worked out of our house so he was always around, I was very close to him. My mother was very intelligent and had a post-graduate degree which she never used. If she had been born a generation later, I think she would have been a happier person because motherhood and homemaking were not her thing. My parents had a real active social life, there were always people around. In grade school, I was a very good student, but as I got older, I liked to socialize more, did just enough to skim by on B's and C's.

My younger years were good, but the older I got, the more alcohol became a problem for my mother. It seems she never adjusted to being away from her family and her girlhood home. Every summer we would visit my grandmother in Wisconsin; I loved that and when my mother had her act together, there wasn't anyone I wouldn't rather be with—she was witty, smart and fun, just on top of everything. Gradually, she went downhill—two or three martinis at lunch...she wouldn't show up for things—like at school or her job.

By the time I was in high school, everyone knew about my mother. Like most teenagers, I was sensitive to how people live and what people think of you. My mother's drinking couldn't be hidden and I hated her for what she was doing to our family. She had a super husband, three healthy, intelligent kids—none of us were ever in any serious trouble. She had it all, I thought—and was trashing it. I believe alcoholism is an addiction, but it's easier for someone on the outside to say that and to think you should feel sorry for the alcoholic than it is to be living in the situation. When I look back, some things are not a big deal now—like your mother not showing up for your graduation—but they sure were important then.

When things got too bad at home, I would go somewhere else. I sort of had surrogate mothers all over. In spite of Mom's alcoholism, my father kept us three kids reassured. He was the rudder, trying to keep everything together. The summer before my senior year, I met a boy who was my first serious relationship, but he was going away to college. Keeping up the relationship with the distance between us was too difficult, so it didn't work out; then I got involved with someone who was using me to make another girl jealous. That wasn't a good situation, not a lot of ego strokes for me when he finally dumped me to marry her in the spring of '62.

Back then my social life was the most important thing to me. Really, I had no character, no backbone. I graduated from high school and my personal life went to pot. In June, my father had a heart attack and died. In fact, he was buried on my 20th birthday—that was the beginning of everything falling apart, literally and physically, my family drifted.

I didn't have enough education to get a decent job and my mother went downhill fast. We would get calls from the police station and have to go get her, it was horrible. My oldest brother was married while I wasn't stable at all. One day in November a friend and I were sitting around, it was raining and very gray. We called a friend who had moved to California and was living on a houseboat; she said, "Come on out!"

We threw our stuff in the car and left notes for our mothers and off we went! It was absolutely crazy. My friend had this little MG which she drove through the Rockies—at one point in a blizzard. We stopped for gas, this lady came out of a log cabin, crying and crying...it was the day of President Kennedy's assassination. It seemed to me like society was in upheaval as well as my own life. The wonder of it is that I didn't get involved with drugs because California was like a different culture to me, a very naive midwestern girl. I had no idea what people were talking about or what was going on—a lot was simply over my head.

Eventually we ended up outside San Diego, two girls living in an apartment on the beach, we held a lot of parties. A sign of the times! When a party was on, anyone who wandered by, wandered in...I had too much to drink, a lot is pretty foggy, but one turned out to be a very expensive party for me. Today I think it would be called date rape, but back then it was called being a loose woman. Because of the drinking, I wasn't myself, I was really pretty far gone. I remember his first name, recognized him as someone who lived further up the beach, probably about the same age as me—20.

He was a big guy, blonde and an artist. He wasn't really attractive, but when you are drunk, everyone is attractive. I know I had relations with him, never saw him again. If I hadn't been drinking, I'm sure I wouldn't have been for the sex part. I didn't really know much about sex, mostly misinformation. Birth control? What was that—back then? It is so different now—in a way that's good, in a way it's not. It's good there is information available, but experimenting is not good, even today.

When I realized I was pregnant, I panicked, left California and went back home. I knew a girl who had once confided in me that she had gone away and had a baby, so I got in touch with her to find out where I could go to have my baby. Abortion never entered my mind. The home for unwed mothers was in Ohio, but there was a waiting list; by the time I got in, I was showing, so people in my hometown knew. My brother drove me there and dropped me off.

The home was attached to a hospital for women where we all worked and it was staffed by nuns. About 16 girls lived in the home, ranging in age from 14 to 31. Every situation you could possibly imagine was there. We supported each other; there was always someone you could talk to, but I wouldn't say we had formal counseling. If someone was down, we all tried to help her out of it. I think the jobs we had in the hospital were good because it kept us busy. I worked for a nun who wasn't too much older than I—though I called her Simon Legree, we had a lot of fun together. To this day, I write and visit her.

No one from my family ever came to see me. My mom was supposed to come one day. I got up, did my hair and everything, but my brother called, said she wasn't coming. She was drunk anyhow and I didn't want her there that way. I hated her for what I felt she had done to our family, blaming her for my father's death. She was a big factor in why I never considered keeping my baby. I wouldn't even have been able to trust her to hold a baby. It was impossible to tell when she was sober.

Of course, all of us in the home had the option to change our minds up to the last minute, but I don't remember any discussion by the nuns or priests or doctors about how being a parent would work. We were very well taken care of—physically. Emotionally, the experience was made as comfortable as possible. We were all self-conscious to leave the hospital, to go out into society pregnant. One lovely woman invited all of us to her home in the country for a picnic. That was very nice, a kindness I've always remembered.

At one point, my oldest brother offered to raise my baby. I thought that would be too painful for me and, frankly, he and his wife didn't have the kind of situation I wanted for my child. They had married too young and had children too fast. My other brother was away at college. There was no social support system—no day care centers. I could earn only a minimum wage and I didn't want that kind of life for my child. Why should she suffer?

The hardest part was when my baby was born. After delivery, a nun took me up once to see her; I could have held her then, but I didn't dare. When she was two days old, a social worker came, asked me what her name was. I gave her an Irish name and my father's name for a middle name. I was so pleased to be able to name her. When I told my mother I had a girl, she said something to the effect that was "better than a boy." I can't tell you how mad that made me, how upset—as though it was O.K. to give a daughter away but not a son.

I wanted to say, "This is not only your granddaughter

you're talking about, this is your daughter you're talking to." I already knew she favored boys, that she didn't want to have any other children after my brothers, but putting it into words like that still upsets me. My father was the one who wanted a daughter.

I didn't receive a birth photo or any information about my baby or the family who adopted her, except for their religion. I left the home with another girl's parent who took me to my mother's home. For a while, I just hung around, then I got a job. The first year was very hard for a lot of reasons. Living with my mother was awful; my brother's wife had a baby a month before mine and, in our small town, there was a lot of talk. People knew I had been pregnant and I was much more sensitive than I am now.

Finally, I got a room by myself—no cooking facilities and only a half bath, but I couldn't take living with my mother. I had no medical insurance, lived on saltines and orange juice. It was a very bare existence. When I had a date, the best thing was going out to dinner! I met the man who would be my first husband—Lee. We started as buddies. I didn't find him physically attractive, but he had a good sense of humor. He'd heard the rumor too that I'd had a baby—that was hard. Lee invited me to spend Easter with his family—it was them I fell in love with!

As soon as I walked in Lee's parents' door, it was like I was wrapped in a warm blanket. They were the family I always wanted! From that point on, we dated, then eventually we slept together and felt we should get married. Looking back now, I think, "My God, why?" At the time, though, we did have fun together and I guess I convinced myself that we had similar outlooks, a similar sense of humor, and that it would be a good match. However, it was not.

At the age of 29 I was diagnosed with cancer. Lee

and I had one son, and since I thought I was going to die, I didn't want him to grow up alone. I put an operation off until I got pregnant again. This wasn't easy because the relationship between Lee and me was not good, but I did have a second son and then a hysterectomy. The night I got home from the hospital, Lee bawled me out, said he would never sleep with me again since I could no longer have children and that he would only stay with me until our youngest son was 18. Then we would divorce.

I believed him. After 12 years of living with him, I had some sort of breakdown, huddled in the corner all day crying, unable to take care of myself. I got scared. On my own I went to a psychologist and, through that whole process, I got up the courage to get a divorce myself. It was like I came out of a long dark tunnel of 10 or 15 years' duration.

I started back to work and sometime before the divorce was final, about eight months, I was promoted to branch manager of a bank and had a decent income, not great, but for the first time in my life, I was handling my life. I was going to school at night, coping with the kids and felt wonderful. Lee had fits, wanted his whole family to hate me like he did. He was very bitter. His mother said, "I'm afraid for you." He threatened to kill me, said it would be worth 70 years in prison to see me dead. Eventually he left the state.

My mother died when she was 61—when I was still married to Lee. She looked like she was 85, was in diapers and pretty much out of control. I never trusted her to even hold my sons. She could be violent; got to the point where she set fires and there was no place that could care for her except a mental institution. We had a family pow-wow—what to do with Mom? My oldest brother took on the responsibility, even carried her to the bathroom...all while trying to raise five kids.

It was unbearable. I feel alcohol has robbed me of a mother and a normal family life.

After my divorce, I was very cautious. I didn't go to singles bars, would only go out with somebody that someone else I could trust knew. When I met Sam, I thought it was too easy. No one finds the right person that easy, so I backed off. My brother told me, "Well, don't hold it against the guy." Sam had been divorced for three years, had one son. He encouraged me to date others for a while, so from time to time I did—but no one measured up to Sam. After a couple of years dating, we married.

This year we had our 13th anniversary. Sam knows about my daughter, my sons don't. Eventually, I will tell them because of the health factors, but my youngest is 17, at a stage where he thinks he is perfect and no one else is. He's very judgmental right now. Sam is very supportive, thinks it would be wonderful if I could meet my daughter, but I signed a contract and the decision has to come from her.

I don't think it is right for pregnant youngsters to keep their babies. Their mothers and fathers end up raising the child, which isn't good for anyone. There are many families who would love to have children. When one of my nieces became pregnant as a teenager, her father asked me, "What do you think?" I said I wouldn't hesitate a moment about adoption, I feel that strongly. Even if there is a good economic situation, being a single parent is very difficult and not fair to the baby.

The stress is tremendous; there is no time for yourself and it is not healthy for everything to revolve around the child. There has to be a balance that I don't believe you can get as a single parent. Murdering a child through abortion isn't right either. I did what I felt was best for my daughter and I don't regret my decision, it was right for her and for me. I miss her. I would give anything to have been able to watch her grow up, I would give anything to see her now, to be a small part of her life.

PAULA

"It's embarrassing, being in the hospital and everybody knows you're going to put your kid up for adoption."

In her small, neat apartment 25-year-old Paula talked of her decision to place two infant daughters, born a year apart, for adoption. Her first born, Jermaine, was in school. As a single parent and a black woman, Paula was struggling to provide a good environment for Jermaine and did not feel she could handle two, much less three children. When her second and third children were born, she placed them for adoption. Since the black community has a long history of informal adoption between family members, Paula stubbornly endured the disapproval of brothers and sisters—isolating herself as much as possible.

A soft spoken woman, Paula told her caseworker that she did not know the identity of her babies' father when in fact she was in a long-term relationship with the three children's father, Rene. While he objected to Paula's decision, he did not interfere nor was he able to offer the economic security Paula sought. Before she signed relinquishments, approximately two weeks after each daughter's birth, Paula asked to hold the baby one last time. Her biggest concern was that there would be no homes for her daughters, having been told by the first agency she contacted that there were no approved black families.

Since the placements, Paula learned from her caseworker that each of her birthdaughters was being raised as the only child of a single black woman. She was pleased to receive two or three photos for a period of two years from each adoptive mother.

There were nine of us, but I was like an only child because I was the baby, my brother closest to me was 10 years older. It was me, my mom and dad after my brother graduated from high school and went into the Army. We lived in the country. My parents were from

Arkansas, came north for better jobs and were headed to Cleveland. They stopped here where some relatives lived and stayed put. My father built our house, then he died when I was eight years old, so it was my mom and me left.

It was a pretty good life because she got social security and a pension from my father. We didn't really have too much to worry about. I went to a country school, got B's and C's and grew up with a lot of whites. From third grade on, I was always in some kind of choir and wanted to be a singer, but I was too scared—have always been like that—you know, shy.

As I was growing up, my mom was sick a lot and couldn't teach me about life like maybe she should have. I was with her a lot when I wanted to be with my friends, but she had to stay in bed and someone had to be with her. Basically, I raised myself from the time I was 14. An older sister came to live with us for a while and said, "Mom, Paula's a teenager. She needs to be out, you know." I was pretty naive, dated a little at age 15 or 16, but I never brought the boyfriend home. My mom didn't know anything about it.

At school, I was pretty popular with the boys. Then I met Rene and we went together for a year. We broke up because he was more serious than I was, but after I graduated from high school, we began seeing each other again. I wasn't sexually active until I was 19, then I didn't use any birth control and got pregnant. Rene proposed to me, but I said no because he wasn't ready really to be a father. That was 1986 and, in 1987, my mother died before Jermaine was born. She didn't like Rene because his background was very different, his family was poor. None of my brothers and sisters liked him either. Rene had trouble keeping a job and he had gotten himself expelled before he graduated, so he wasn't making good money.

First I thought about abortion, but I couldn't see killing a person. Maybe it's just an organism, but an organism made by two living people is a living thing, a person too. I thought about adoption and went to see a counselor in another city because I didn't know how my family would feel about adoption. Three of my sisters had babies out of wedlock and when I told them I was planning on giving mine up, one said, "I don't think you should do it because none of us have never did that." She made me feel guilty.

When I got further along, I could feel the baby move. I remember one time when I was at the beautician, I was getting my hair done, and I seen my stomach, it was moving back and forth. I thought, "Isn't that neat? That is really nice!" I kind of accepted it more after that.

Once Jermaine was born, I came home wondering, "How am I going to support this child?" Rene wasn't working and his family didn't help out at all. My sister saw the expression on my face and said, "Things are going to be okay. It has some ups and downs, but everything's going to be all right."

I got on Aid to Families of Dependent Children. I had wanted to study nursing after high school, go to college, but I didn't do it. Even though Rene's family didn't like me and mine didn't like him, we still saw each other. While I took the pill for two years, I had problems with it, had the medication changed and in between, I got pregnant again. Rene wasn't too thrilled either, proposed to me though and I said no again because I didn't want to tie myself to him. If he couldn't support Jermaine, he couldn't support me and another baby, couldn't do right by any of us, that's what I thought.

This time I actually called an abortion clinic. The lady said to come in, there might be protestors out there—just to ignore them. I couldn't have people looking at me that way so I went to an adoption agency. No one from our families knew—just Rene and me. And he wasn't too happy about it. I was pretty clear about adoption. In the hospital, when my little girl was born, a couple of nurses told me they admired me for choosing adoption, but they also said, "I couldn't do it personally..." That was the hardest part, the staff knowing that you're doing something they couldn't do!

When you're a single parent, you never have enough money to get what you need. I had to think of Jermaine, he was into the "I want" stage and needing things. While I don't want him to be spoiled, I tell him "no" about some things, I want to be able to get him nice things too. Money is the hardest part for me. My car is always breaking down, making it hard for me to get around. Out in the country there is no public transportation, so when I think of my goals, of getting into nurses training, it makes it hard to put it all together.

I worked for a while and a lady, who was also black, had a teenager who became pregnant. She was going to make her get an abortion. I said, "Adoption would be better, not as painful as killing is." Especially if a girl is underage, she shouldn't be a mother, but, you know, everyone has their own situation and has to do what they think is right. There is something about black people and family which I think goes back to slavery. I don't know any other black girl who put a baby up for adoption like I did. That first time, it was secret, but when I got pregnant a third time, my family knew; they were on my case all the time.

I named the second little girl Shanay and almost kept her. I wanted a little girl, but it was the wrong time. Rene still couldn't hold a job, his family still ignored Jermaine, who was almost four. A lot of pressure came from my family while I was in the hospital. My sister went over to Rene's house and told everyone there I was going to put the baby up for adoption, which was none of her business or theirs. They never offered any help anyhow.

One of my sisters who had an abortion asked, "How can you do that?" They all made me feel like I was really bad and there was something so special about Shanay that I almost changed my mind the day the social worker came to the hospital. I had held both girls, changed their diapers and all, but I was more attached to Shanay. Rene came to the hospital. He was mad, started talking about getting back both baby girls. I told him, "You can't do that. I signed papers already. You are their father, but you aren't being a father to them."

The only thing I'm worried about is that the baby girls will someday be mad at me for putting them up for adoption. I'm scared of that. One day they may want to know who I am. I would be glad to meet them. They will be welcome here. I know I will always think of them, but I will not look for them myself. I would not interrupt their lives, but if they want to know me and do it on their own, that would be fine. I gave pictures of myself for them.

As Jermaine gets older, I will tell him about his sisters. We all have birthdays with the number "4" in the month or the date, all kind of together. Every birthday I wonder what the girls are doing and what they look like. I use birth control now. I didn't mean to get pregnant and I can't let it happen again. It was my own fault, but I tried to do it all the best way I knew how.

My sister said to me, "I heard you put some kids up for adoption. Why didn't you keep them or have an abortion?" I told her what I did was better for them. Then my brother says, "You know what you done? It was wrong!"

When they point their fingers like that, I said, "How can you tell me what I am to do? You have kids of your own—be a parent to your own kids, you have enough trouble there without getting into my business."

What I would do different if I could? I would go to college or get some training right after high school. I would have a good career, a good job. I would have no kids.

CONNIE

"He wrote to me, said he wanted us to be together; he wanted me and our baby, but it was too late, she was gone."

A medical crisis at the age of 40 was the stimulus for Connie to search aggressively for the daughter she placed for adoption 21 years before. Despite a successful career as a professional ice skater and making the transition from worldwide travel to teaching at a local rink, Connie seems to down-play the successes in her life. She feels very strongly that an adoption placement for her baby was not her choice. She also carries the burdens of guilt and anger that she was unable to come up with a better solution herself.

Several months after this interview, Connie's birthdaughter responded to her letter. With the support of her search group, Connie is preparing for their reunion with great anticipation.

❧

I did what was required of me by the society of the 1960s. There was no choice, no decision. It was drilled into my head that adoption was the only answer, the noble and right thing for me to do. Society was so different back then. If you were pregnant, you were a bad girl, you brought shame on yourself, your family and your church. It was like someone said: "You got yourself into trouble and this is how we are going to get you out of it. We are going to send you away; you are going to give your baby up. That is what happens to bad girls."

It was the night of my senior prom—1966. Skip and I had grown up in the same neighborhood, were dating and I trusted him. I was young, 18, naive and dumb. Really, I didn't even know what "it" was as far as sex went. Skip kept saying, "Don't worry, Connie. I would never do *that* to you." Since he wasn't doing "it," I figured whatever he was doing was O.K. By the time I figured out what "it" was, I was pregnant. Stupid! Stupid! It's the way things were back then.

When I started throwing up, I had a feeling that something was wrong. By that point, Skip had joined the Marines and left town and I was at the start of my freshman year in college. It was frightening. I remember that cartoon of Snoopy laying on top of his dog house and the caption is, "No problem is so big or so complicated that it can't be totally ignored." That's what I did—I ignored it because I didn't know how to deal with it. I didn't tell my best friend or my mom. Finally I wrote Skip. His basic training would be completed around Christmas, he would have five days off and he planned to come home. Then we were going to talk about "our little problem" as he called it. Skip knew he was going to Vietnam, but he wanted us to get married. He apologized, saying he felt he had raped me. I think that if our parents hadn't gotten involved we would probably have worked it out together.

When I was about seven months pregnant, I went to the doctor for the first time because I had hives and terrible itching. The baby's waste was backing up into my system, a kind of toxic poisoning caused by the pregnancy. I went to my family doctor, gave a fake name, but one of the nurses was a friend of my mom's, though she didn't recognize me at first.

The other nurse said, "You're not married...what are you going to do? You are going to have to make some decision because this child could be born any day." Than I told the doctor my real name and they recognized my family. The nurse called my mom. She did a good job of telling her because my mom tends to have a hysterical nature, but the nurse handled it great:

"Connie has a real problem and we have to support her, stand beside her. She is pregnant, almost at term, so if we do anything to upset her, she might have the child right away. We don't know what to do until you make some decisions."

That day I went home, stayed in bed, and my mom sat down on the edge, crying, "I thought you were getting a little bit heavy, but I knew you hadn't been out with anyone for months. I never dreamed you could be so far pregnant."

My dad never said much to me at all—he's the silent type. My mom told me things he supposedly said or did, like he was at work one day and got so upset that he went behind one of the machines and was crying. One of the guys came up to him and said, "What's the matter?" And Dad just said, "Please leave me alone." A generation before his sister had gotten pregnant, a rape situation, and the shame on the family was so great until they found an older gentleman who agreed to marry her, to give the baby a name and take the shame off of them.

Mom asked me who the baby's father was. At first I told her, "It doesn't matter," but then I told her and she went right down the street to talk to Skip's mother. She put all the blame on Skip; he told me that later in a letter. He said, "How can I marry you when your parents think I'm the worst person on earth?" He wanted to send me money and his parents wanted to adopt the baby and move out of state.

My parents got jealous then or felt left out, saying it wouldn't be fair that his parents got to raise the baby the way they wanted to. It was their first grandchild too! They wanted the best possible home for the baby. They told me they found a good adoption agency out of the state where the prospective parents were screened thoroughly. So they whisked me away. I remember they said, "We can never let your grandparents find out about this or we will never hear the end of it."

My father told my brothers and my sister that I was pregnant. The only reaction was as though they never heard it. I was told I had to be very good at this home. If I wasn't, the agency wouldn't place the child, then I would "be stuck with it" and what would we do? I felt like I had really screwed up totally with my life; I had brought a terrible shame upon my family.

I was sent to a home for "unwed mothers" where I was in a room with eight other girls, all of us graduated from high school. Altogether, 76 girls were in the home, ranging from 12 years old to 26. We all had our jobs to keep the place clean and the younger girls went to school. I worked in the laundry. The saying was that the laundry girls "went down" first, meaning down to the delivery room because we had to carry big, heavy baskets of drapes from the hospital, full of blood and afterbirth.

The second night at the home, we had a Valentine's party. They divided everybody up into groups, then they gave us a nursery rhyme and we had to change the nursery rhyme into a Valentine's song. I can remember that it was very hard to do. The group that won sang to "Mary Had a Little Lamb":

"Mary had a boyfriend, boyfriend, boyfriend
Mary had a boyfriend he said he loved her true;
told her that he loved her so, loved her so, loved her so,
told her that he loved her so, she ended up at Booth."

Everybody was laughing and applauding and I sat there and cried. I said, "Oh my God, these people are laughing at this. This is horrible." I hadn't begun to come to terms with my situation. Once a week a counselor would come in; we'd talk and she would ask, "Can you imagine what kind of a family you would like your child to go to? Can you describe this family for me? Would you want your baby to live in the city or the country?"

It seemed as though whatever I answered, she said, "This is like the family we have for you." I didn't know if their list of families was so big that I could say, choose what I wanted, or if she was trying to pacify me. Once she took me out for a hot fudge sundae and then to an ice skating rink. I was watching all the kids skate and said, "It would be so neat to be able to do that."

She remarked, "Once this is over with and forgotten, you *will* be able to do that." Then she started with, "Maybe you should choose a goal for your life so you'll be able to forget what you've been through. You need a goal. Why don't you make skating your goal and see what you can do with it?" Then she asked, "What's the biggest dream in skating?" And I said, "Gee—maybe skating in the Ice Capades." She said, "Make *that* your goal."

From that point I really decided to push myself into skating, to do something to make my parents proud of me. I don't know why I didn't think I could go back to college; instead, skating became my life.

About a month after I entered the home, I delivered—early by a few weeks. They asked me if it was going to be "natural childbirth" and I said, "Yea—okay," thinking that natural childbirth meant vaginal delivery rather than a C-section. I didn't know what it really meant! I thought when my time came, they would give me a gas mask, I would wake up later when it was all over. I didn't know *how* I would know when my time came! I honestly did not know about labor and no one prepared me.

One night I woke up, having to go to the bathroom...but I couldn't, so I went to the hospital floor and asked the nurse for a laxative. "Why don't we check you out," she said. "You're in labor," she announced and put me in a room full of lights. I didn't know what the heck was going on. I kept yelling, "It's hurting again, what am I going to do? Help me." Finally she said, "Would you quit bothering me, I've got a lot of paperwork to do—just leave me alone!" Then she shut the door and went out. It was in the middle of the night, it was dark and I was afraid. I kept screaming. In the morning, someone asked me what I wanted to name the baby if it was a boy, and what name if it was a girl. I started having another pain right then, couldn't talk, and the person said, "It doesn't matter because they are going to change the name anyway."

No one was nice to me there. The doctor came in, looked at my fingernails, grabbed my hand and said, "Why haven't we cut these fingernails?" I remember that was one of the rules, when you are in term—short fingernails.

Another lady came in, a nurse, very fat, and said to me very sternly, "I've always found that when I had my children it was a lot easier if you relax and don't tense up like that." Only she didn't say *how* I was supposed to relax!

My daughter weighed 7 lbs. 4 oz. and I named her Danielle. I was not allowed to hold her until after I signed the adoption papers. After she was born they put her in an incubator. She was off to my left, on the other side of the room, and I kept looking over at her.

Later they let me go down to the nursery and look at her through the window, twice a day, every day, but they would not let me hold her. My father sent me a dozen red roses—that was his biggest expression about the situation. I wanted to take a picture of her, but they wouldn't let me.

On the day I was to sign the papers, the caseworker took me into a little room and asked, "Would you like to hold your baby for a few minutes?"

I said, "Of course." It was so weird that this caseworker, this woman who I thought was my friend, was all at once very businesslike. Once I put my name on that line, it was hurry up, Connie, we have things to do with the baby! The caseworker told me the couple already had a four-year-old boy; that the adoptive mother had been born without a uterus so they had planned a family by adoption from the start and that they would tell my daughter too that she was adopted. That was all!

I held Danielle, put her foot up to my fingers, measuring it. It was the length of my little finger. I knew I was always going to remember that. I was crying and a tear fell on her cheek. When the caseworker took her out of my arms, I whispered, "Goodbye, I promise I'll see you again someday." I said a prayer to God, asking him to take care of her for me. Then I sat there for a while, struck with grief. For the first time, I felt the emptiness that would stay with me from that point on. Staring out the window, I saw the caseworker, crossing the parking lot, carrying Danielle. She went to a green, 1967 Mustang with a black vinyl top. I watched her strap Danielle in a carrier, get in the car and drive away.

The next day I left the home, on Good Friday. My mom's biggest worry had been Easter Sunday. What would she say to all the relatives if I wasn't present? When my parents picked me up, I realized what a toll it had been on them. My mom looked 15 years older. She was relieved that I was home for Easter dinner with no one the wiser. Sack dresses were popular then, my mom went out and bought me one. So there I was fashionably attired like nothing had happened.

Secrecy was so important. Even the doctor had said to me, "I stitched you up so nobody will ever be able to tell you've had a baby." The first thing I asked to do at home was redecorate my bedroom with new curtains, bedspreads and I painted. Then I found a job at the telephone company and I began taking ice skating lessons. I poured all my energy into practice, took private training where I had to travel two hours back and forth. Skip still wrote me letters, asking me to please write back, that he would do anything to try to get our baby back, but it was too late. I knew there was no chance of getting Danielle back. I never answered Skip's letters.

After six months I called the agency and asked for any information that they could give me about Danielle. I had misunderstod them because I was thinking that once the adoption was finalized, they would tell me how the baby was. Instead the caseworker was very icy. "Connie, I certainly cannot give you information except that your baby is very happy, very healthy." I felt I had been tricked. No one had prepared me for the pain and emotional trauma of giving away my own flesh and blood.

The message was: "Forget. Get on with your life." But I didn't forget. I wondered about Danielle all the time. On her birthdays, I would freak out. Later when I was successful in my skating, was a professional skater, I would place a personal ad in the newspaper, "Happy birthday—from your birthmother," or "God bless you, darling daughter—from your birthmother." I felt I had to reach out to her.

Whenever I flew into Chicago, I'd look out over the lights of the city, thinking, "She's out there somewhere." I wanted to start knocking on doors to find her! I remember a train trip, after I was travelling as a professional skater, when I started thinking about Danielle, had too much wine and I lay on the floor, sobbing, "She's gone, she's gone—oh God." Sometimes the pain came out in my drinking too much, eating too much. I went through terrible depression.

I accomplished my goal in skating but I didn't feel good as a person. Relationships with men were difficult for me—it was three years before I even dated. Once I was engaged, but when I told the guy about my baby, the relationship dissolved. Another time I was close to a man whose first girlfriend had been at the same home I was at the same time! He recalled going to visit her and that helped bring us closer together for a while. But over 25 years, I never married. The man I'm involved with now is very supportive of my decision to search for Danielle.

My motivation resulted after I found out at the age of 40 that I needed a hysterectomy, that cancer was a possibility. I felt, "She is the only child I'm ever going to have and I have to try to find her." I joined an adoption support group and when I gave my history, everyone encouraged me to search. When I recontacted the agency, they kept putting me off. I wondered what my daughter had been told about me through the years—or did she imagine that I was a whore or an indecent mother? What if she wanted nothing to do with me?

The support group had members from the entire adoption triad—birthparents, adoptees and adoptive parents. One wonderful adoptive mother said she'd like to give a hug to the birthmother of each of her children for all the joy they'd given her! Some parents were searching as a 21st birthday tribute to give their child all the information they'd wondered about. Finally a woman said to me, "I have a name for you to call, a person who can give you all the names of children born on a particular day." This person was a computer hacker and also an adoptee who vowed to find his birthparents and to help others.

With his information, he was eventually able to narrow the search down to nine babies born on Danielle's birthdate in the city I was in—nine babies who were placed for adoption. Then he was able to narrow it further to four babies who were placed by agencies. He could access information by having figured out the codes. Then I went to a genealogist who said, "Let's see what we can do with this!" With her help, I was able to eliminate one possibility by looking through all the high school yearbooks in the city—the eye and hair coloring didn't match up. On the second possibility, I got lucky—I put the pictures side by side with the high school ones of me and Skip and they matched so much it was frightening! From the freshman to senior year, I could tell she battled her weight like I did—and from a sports team picture, I could see she had my thighs—Skip's eyes.

Still—I had no proof this girl was my birthdaughter. I wrote to the birth records department, saying my name was so and so and I needed a long copy of my birth certificate. I sent a cashier's check. When I told the support group, they said I could get into trouble for signing a name that wasn't mine. I was scared about it—figured I'd get a letter saying I committed a crime or they were coming after me. Two days before I was scheduled for surgery an official envelope arrived; I couldn't open it, I was so frightened.

My boyfriend opened the envelope for me—it was a birth certificate, the time of birth matched exactly what I remembered; the doctor's name matched too. That proved it to me! My boyfriend was angry at the system. He said, "This isn't fair. The birth certificate makes it look like the adoptive parents *gave birth* to her and that isn't true!" I was just happy that I could go into surgery with positive feelings. I had found her!

Later I had to think about this very real person and what she could go through if my search was a complete shock to her. What if she hated me? I knew the town she had grown up in; through all those years, I had gone there to visit a particular little deli, never realizing she was there too. With a friend from my support group, I drove past the house she grew up in, feeling very guilty for invading her privacy. I even wore a blonde wig so there would be no similarity if she would happen to see me! I knew I was nothing to her, just someone that she knew existed. I'm not her parent, I'm not a friend. I wondered if she hated me for giving her chunky legs.

For 25 years Danielle was with me in my mind and there was a void in my life. I have no idea what she was told about me or how she feels, but I want a chance, a chance finally to know her. Through an intermediary I wrote her a letter.

The receipt from the registered letter I sent her came back—then I waited and waited, wondering if it was the wrong time in her life for me to make contact or what. I know some adopted children aren't curious about their birthparents until they have children of their own. My letter out of the blue had to have been a big shock. What if her response was, "My God, who is this person? Do I want anything to do with her?" I tried to prepare myself for no answer—or a blunt, "Leave me alone. I have a life of my own." What if her parents were upset to know she was interested in answering and to avoid hurting them, she was silent?

I am still waiting. It will kill me inside if I never hear from her, but at least I know some things about her life. Maybe that's all I'll ever have, knowing that I gave her life and did the only thing for her that I could do at the time. Until I began going to the search support, I couldn't even say the words "adoptive parents," I couldn't think of them except to say "those people who are taking care of her." Now I can feel that they gave her a good life, a good education, and would like to be able to thank them.

Adoption today is very different. If a woman decides she absolutely cannot care for her child and can choose to have communication with the adoptive parents, that is better than knowing nothing. I really believe there should be at least a thin thread of communication through the years so the birthmother knows the baby is okay. She is not going to forget ever that she gave up her own flesh and blood. Ten, 20 years later, she is still going to wonder about that child.

For me—if I could go back in time, I would not have given my daughter away. My life has been hell because of it. My relationships with men, my feelings about myself have been affected. Years of psychotherapy, a successful career—nothing has helped erase the agony. Adoption was not the answer. I don't feel I was ever given a choice. I was told what to do and I was too young, too naive to question it.

I loved my baby, I held her once. And I have never forgotten.

SARAH

"It is real frustrating from the birthmother's point of view because it feels like you are the forgotten one and that is very sad, that adoption happens that way."

In the small town hospital where Sarah gave birth to her son in 1990, the administrative staff refused to honor the "temporary release" Sarah signed in order for her caseworker to move the baby into foster care. Because of her difficult labor and complications, Sarah wasn't to be released at the same time as her child and she wasn't able to sign a permanent relinquishment of parental rights in the hospital. In a wheelchair, with her newborn in her lap, Sarah was pushed through the hospital lobby by a nurse—into the parking lot and there she handed her baby to her caseworker.

Sarah read letters from several couples, hoping to select one that seemed to meet her criteria which she specified in writing: "They must be Christian...open minded...with good communication between themselves and not believe in physical punishment. Family must be important to them and I prefer they be open to the needs of their birthmother, being free to share photos and letters. This, I think, is a small gift to share compared to the gift of a child."

Before her birthson was two years old, Sarah learned from her caseworker that the adoptive parents considered their obligation to her over. It was not the kind of relationship Sarah anticipated. She writes, "I wanted my son to have a complete home which I could not give him. Because I love him, I want him to be whole in his heart. I have a dream that someday—even if he is an adult—that I will be able to hold him in my arms again. I would like him to know the love I will always hold for him."

ઙ

My parents were farmers, though my father also worked in construction. For a while we raised Herefords so I've always been used to hard work. There were eight of us kids, ranging from 17 years to me—the baby. Five boys and three girls. I guess I have small town values, Christian values, a toss-up between the Baptist church and the Quakers. I've been to both and consider myself either. If my parents hadn't always been around for me, to help me through bad times, I don't know where I would be today.

It seems like I've always been a "yes" person, giving up what I wanted, giving up myself. While I hold myself responsible for that, I'm still (at 37 years of age) trying to get my life on track. While I was in high school, I had a boyfriend I was real fond of, but he was killed in a car accident. I was still in high school, 16 years old, when I met Rich. He was 28 years old and the brother of my brother's wife. Rich worked for my dad and already had two kids, a nine-year-old son and a younger daughter from his first marriage.

We dated for three years. I've always wondered why nobody in the family stepped in to say, "He's too old for you," or told me some of the things I found out later that they must have known. My brother tried to but no one ever actually said, "You can't date him." Probably I would have listened at first, then gone ahead anyway! The age gap was too great!

A year after my high school graduation, Rich and I got married and moved to a dairy farm. He loved working with cows but wasn't very good at following instructions from other people. I learned he'd been kicked out of the Navy, though for a while he was in the Reserves and could have gone on to become an officer. He chose cows without asking me my opinion. There I was with two stepkids at age 18! In the beginning, we were happy. I've always liked animals, so when Rich decided to put all our money into a farm, it was okay with me.

In five years we lost everything, our investment, our herd, and we gained two more children, Jason and Carmen. There were things that weren't under our control entirely that led to the farm loss. We had to move in with my parents, living off them while I nagged Rich to get a job. From state to state, he travelled, building dryer bins for seed corn companies. I only saw him from midnight Friday to Sunday noon when he left again. That didn't help matters any. He never helped with the kids, in fact, he totally ignored me because he wanted a dairy farm, to be a herdsman no matter what it took or what I thought.

Finally I told him, "I'm sick of living like this, what do you want?" Rich brought out a magazine with "help wanted" ads on dairy farms. He applied for a position in Pennsylvania, which looked real good on paper. Being an adventurous person, I agreed to go and he got the job. When we made the move, it was awful. While the farm owner's house was nice, the one we lived in was filthy; the floors were swayed and there was no heat, no hot water, no stove or refrigerator and no beds to sleep on. They expected us to work ungodly hours. Their milking herd was 87 cows plus a herd of Herefords and calves.

All these animals were in one barn, big enough to hold 70 cows, so they were jammed in every corner. We had to keep switching cows around, they'd get loose—there were no doors on the barn—and out they'd go. We had to feed them high moisture corn twice a day—200 cows. Since there was no unloader in the silo, it had to be done by hand, by shovel. After six weeks without a day off, I told Rich, "This is it. We are not going to do this anymore!"

We called the agency, told them about the poor conditions and insisted they find us a new position or we would just leave. The second farm in Pennsylvania was better, the house was nice and the people had a real Christian outlook. I didn't have to milk and could spend time with the kids. Only Rich had such a poor attitude, if he didn't like something they told him to do, he would tell them so. Eventually he got fired. With no savings, barely enough money to buy gas, we drove our camper and pickup truck back to my parents' home.

It seems like my history is to learn things the hard way! After a week at my parents', Rich was still looking for another herdsman position and found one in Indiana. A widow and her son were running the farm and were willing to pay extra for any work I did. Rich told them we'd take the job, then turned around and accepted a different one in Grand Rapids, Michigan, with a Dutch family. I was so mad at him, especially when they treated us like animals. The job lasted only four months, working conditions were so bad and then we moved in with Rich's grandmother.

I was so emotionally mixed up that I didn't know what was up or down. While Rich never abused me physically, he did mentally. I thought about divorce, actually left him once, years before. I took the kids with all our clothes in garbage bags, but I went back to him. We were living on welfare now and I began taking psychology classes at a local junior college. That was the best thing I ever did for myself, I loved it. Rich took classes too but disagreed with everything I said. It felt like we were going down two seperate roads—he was in his 40s and I was 29, had spent enough years trying to make the marriage work. Finally, I thought, "There isn't anymore to give, I have nothing left."

We separated and I have been battling Rich ever since for child support. I took all four kids, that's about all I got out of the marriage. I found work on a hog farm, was the first woman to do that job and it was hard, 15 to 24 hours a day for a year. There wasn't much money but I had a house to live in and I worked through a lot of anger and grief during that time. Even though I wanted the divorce, it was difficult to fail in a relationship. Eventually I worked in a factory. By this time Jason was 14 years old, Carmen 10. I was working a lot, my friends were married and I had floated around so much through the years that I didn't have much of a social life. The old friends just weren't there.

Rodd was a nice guy who had worked for my dad for 19 years, was always around, but I never dated him. He initiated our relationship. I thought he was a different sort of person, down to earth and independent. He's always doing something, like repairing things, making his own wine. Now I know he's also a big "wuss" (coward), but I didn't find that out until later. He had a seven-year-old daughter from his marriage, Aimee, who lived with him. Unlike Rich, Rodd loved his daughter like crazy, so much that she is a royal brat. She'd get mad at him, haul off and kick him in the knee and talk terribly. I'd tell him, "You can't let Aimee get away with stuff like that. You've got to correct her."

I look back now and I can see the signs, the symptoms that this relationship wasn't going to work, but like I said: I seem to learn the hard way! Rodd never really let go of his marriage. His ex is a crazy woman, but he still is obsessed with her, can't get her out of his head even though she has always treated him like dirt. Other people knew this but no one ever commented on it to me, which makes me mad. Coming from a large family like I do with my sister's husband having gone to school with Rodd, I'd think someone would stand up for me and ask, "You know what he's like?"

Twice I've gotten seriously involved with the wrong person and *afterwards* everyone has an opinion but *beforehand*...no one says a word. I was 36 years old, on contraceptives and got pregnant, a real surprise. Later I had problems with my 16-year-old son, Jason, and he threw that up in my face. "Look," I told him, "I *was* using something, thought I was safe, which just goes to show you that thinking you're protected doesn't mean you are!"

When I told Rodd I was pregnant, that our relationship wasn't strong enough for marriage at that point, he said he needed to do some thinking. I told him, "I won't get married again, knowing it won't last." He went north to hunt, supposedly for 10 days—basically he abandoned me. After six weeks I got hold of him, he wanted me to have an abortion. I thought briefly that it might be the best solution. Then after talking to a friend, I couldn't do it, thought it wouldn't be in line with my Christian beliefs. It was the holiday season, Rodd was taking his ex out while I was sitting at home, waiting for him to call. He didn't have the guts to face me.

By the first of the year, 1991, I was five months along and really hurting financially. My hours at work were cut back, I had three kids to feed with no money. Rodd had thousands of dollars in the bank, I knew that and thought it was pretty crummy, crude that he wouldn't help out. My sister brought up the idea of adoption and my doctor did too at my first appointment. He knew I was single and he had adopted children himself. He also placed babies for adoption right out of his office. I wasn't interested at that point; I was an emotional wreck with all the stuff I learned about Rodd—like he told his ex about us, told his brother that he didn't think the baby was his, anything to cover his butt.

Finally I confronted Rodd. "You have to make a decision one way or the other," I told him. "This is your baby and you're putting me through hell. I'm going through the punishment. I'm the one without work and it's my body going through this." By now I knew Rodd's weak point real well so I threatened him: "You have two choices. You're going to pay the medical expenses and I'll place the baby for adoption. Or I'm going to raise the baby and make you pay ever after."

I was going to make it worthwhile, told him I needed $2,000 cash to cover my expenses. He was upset. "I can't give up my money." He didn't like the idea at all, so I made it very clear that unless I got the money up front, I would get him for child support and everything that he thought belonged to his daughter would belong to this child too. In reality, I didn't know if adoption was what I wanted. Coming from a big family, with my two kids plus stepkids, it was not something ordinarily thought of, but I was determined Rodd was not going to get off scot-free abandoning me.

"When I started dating you, I didn't think you were like this," he told me while writing out a check. I could hardly believe it; for a while we'd eat and pay the bills! Between Rodd and Rich, I was finally sick and tired of having men walk on me. A friend referred me to an adoption agency and I also talked to a lawyer, but I wasn't comfortable with him. I didn't feel he was there for me whereas I could talk with my caseworker about anything. Only I was so emotional that I don't know if she really explained all my options or if she said what she thought I wanted to hear.

While I don't regret making the decision for adoption, I did want a more open adoption than what happened. I don't think it was my caseworker's fault but, looking back, I really thought I'd have pictures and letters for a long time. I should have insisted on meeting the couple, making all of that very clear. I was given the option of one meeting but didn't think at the time I could handle it. Now I wish I had, regardless of how I felt because placing a baby does affect you for the rest of your life. If I had better guidance, some things would have been done differently.

The hardest part of the whole experience was what I went through with my doctor at labor and afterwards. I don't know why he treated me the way he did. My labor was induced and when he checked me, he said, "I'm going home for a little while, you've got a ways to go." The law states that a woman can't be on that medicine without a doctor present, so he turned it off and left for six hours, during which time I was in labor. He returned at midnight, put the medicine back on, which gave me real hard pains and the shakes. Every time I had a contraction my baby's heart rate would drop, then they would give me oxygen and I had to lie in one position the whole time.

For 19 hours, it went on like that—pretty heavy labor and he wouldn't give me anything for pain. Finally, he gave me morphine and the nurse present went nuts, saying to him, "You don't give a pregnant person morphine!" I don't think he treated me right at all. It was terrible. My tailbone was broken during that labor. Long before, I told this doctor I wanted my tubes tied after that delivery. I kind of reminded him of that and he said he wasn't encouraging it. There I was 37 years old, raising four kids and I think I was justified in making that decision.

The doctor remarked, "Don't you think you should wait until you get married and let your husband decide?" I thought: no way. This is my body, my life, my choice. I'm not going to back down. Remember, I'm still in labor while he's standing up, telling me, "Your insurance won't pay for tubals and if you ever want a reversal, I'm the only one in the area who does it." By then he knew I hated his guts, wanted to punch him. When he left the room, the nurse looked at me and said, "My goodness, he does have a problem. He tied my tubes when I was 21 after I only had one child!" She couldn't believe his attitude either!

Maybe it was because I was a single parent or because he was an adoptive parent, I don't know. It sure seemed he was taking something out on me. The whole maternity floor staff knew my baby was being placed for adoption. My son weighed 7 lbs. 13 oz. and I named him Zane. I think I would have been happy raising Zane, but it would have been such a struggle. The other kids would have had to do without things while this way Zane gets what he needs and a couple get a son.

At first I was very open about the adoption. Everybody where I worked knew and if someone asks me about it, I'll tell them, but I don't volunteer anymore. People don't know how to take it. They turn off, or look at you like: "How could you?" or "That's a shame, I couldn't do that." People think a birthmother is uncaring, with no feelings, cold and hard. Once I got really mad at a woman, snapped back at her, "I've had my share of babies, I've raised four kids and if I can do something for someone who can't have any, don't condemn me."

Rodd's mother who is in her 70s knew about Zane and she respects me for my decision even while knowing he is her only grandson. For a long time she was so upset with Rodd she wouldn't talk to him and she told me during the pregnancy that as long as Rodd was carrying a torch for his ex I was out of the picture. She understood why I chose adoption. Rodd's ex is such a looney that while I was in the hospital she poured paint on my car. I knew if I kept Zane, she would try to make my life hell.

My son Jason thought adoption was the best decision while Carmen had little girl fantasies of a baby. I think she's adjusted though. It would have been so very hard to try to raise another child! I go to a birthmother's support group, at first very regularly but then less often. I was suffering because Zane's adoptive parents weren't writing, sent very few pictures. I feel they are really afraid of me. Probably there are cases where that fear is reasonable, but I don't think they understand how I feel.

In my letters, I ask them questions which they never respond to. I sent them a gift which they never commented on—what kind of people are like that? All I hear from them is how "happy Zane is," how "he's never going to want for anything." I know all that. Tell me instead what I asked! It's like they never even read my letter and it takes forever to get a response. I finally resigned myself to that's how it's going to be and quit beating myself with it.

At one point, I was suicidal. If it wasn't for my kids, I probably would have done it, I was so angry—mostly at the doctor. I refused to go back to him for my check-up, tried to schedule with another one and when I was told I'd have to pay extra, I said, "No—that was part of my fee. If something happens to me, you're going to be liable." It took nine weeks before they scheduled me in with another doctor.

It's been over two years now. I don't date. I'm tired of needing help, tired of talking about adoption. It's like I still don't know who I am, I've floated around for so long, I belong nowhere. Ten hours a day, I work. I don't want to go through pain again. I can't change or go back to make sure the adoption was open, which I thought was what I was getting. There's no point to my being angry. If Zane's family ever needed information from me, I'd be happy to provide it, happy they would attempt to make contact. What is scary is that I know they travel a lot, what if I saw them some place? There's no doubt in my mind that I would recognize Zane even if I never get another picture—which is what's going to happen. I would not want to scare them and there'd be no reason for me to talk to them. They would have no idea it was me, I'd just watch them. I wonder what Zane is going to be like when he gets older. Describing my feelings is hard. I look at Zane's pictures, think a lot about him and hope when he's an adult, that he'll look for me. I try to understand how his parents feel; I don't think they understand how I feel and I have to deal with the fact I'll probably never hear from them again. Still—I would do adoption again.

BECKY

"While undergoing radiation treatment, I had to answer all kinds of medical questions. For the first time in my life, I could say 'yes' to my pregnancy. ("Yes, I have a son!") I sat there grinning! It was wonderful."

For more than 25 years, Becky wondered if her son had been placed with a loving family or if he had grown up in a series of foster homes. In the 1960s she had broken not only the taboo of pregnancy without marriage, she had crossed racial lines and fallen in love with a fellow high school student who was black. Though Becky and James married four years after their son was born, they went their separate ways before a first anniversary.

Becky says little about her life as a single woman, that is most of her adult life for she did not marry again until 1991. Shortly thereafter she underwent surgery for breast cancer. Confronting her own mortality, Becky began a search for her birthson, making contact through an agency—first—then with the adoptive parents. Her overtures were well received.

Within a few months, Becky was able to exchange photos, letters—and arrange a meeting with Jed and his parents. Describing the period as "magical," Becky seems to carry no overt anger towards specific persons or resentment at society. Her eyes sparkle when she talks of Jed, who has met her extended family members also. Becky looks forward to an ongoing relationship, as it unfolds, with Jed and his family.

ꟸ

The diagnosis of cancer at 37 pushed me into reality. I had to get all I could out of life, I had to do something to find out what happened to my son. My husband backed me 100 percent though he confessed, "I'm a little afraid because I don't want you to get hurt, to be rejected." I felt I had had enough bumps in life to survive if there were no reaction to my search.

I was raised to believe everybody was equal, but when I acted on that principle, things were reversed a bit. My parents were very strict, sent their five kids to Catholic schools, which were not even integrated by sex in the '60s. The boys were on one side of the school, the girls on the other. I picked out the only black boy in school and he was 16 years old, two years younger than me. He was not my first boyfriend; he was so cute to me! In those days not many people accepted interracial dating, making for a lot of sneaking around.

James and I hung out with a group of public school students, sometimes going to the home of one whose parents were more liberal, more open-minded than most whites were then. Sometimes we'd go to a park to talk. Police were always stopping us, harassing us in cars. We had to duck down so they wouldn't see black and white together. When my parents found out that I was dating James, they didn't like it, wouldn't talk about it or let me bring him to the house.

While the prejudice generally came from whites, James' mom also didn't like our dating, but after a bit she accepted me so we always went to his house. James' family was also Catholic and he was the oldest of two children. After I graduated, I found a job and an apartment with a friend. The neighborhood was predominantly black, though our landlord was white. When he saw James over, he actually threatened me with an axe.

"I don't want any niggers in here!" he yelled. People are small-minded. Close to our apartment was a dance hall, whites went there and sometimes the guys flirted with us. Once James came to the door and when the white guys saw him, they screamed, "nigger lover," and tried to come through the door. I called the police—who came but wrote *me* up for prostitution!

The second or third time James and I had sex, I became pregnant. No birth control. I was very, very frightened, knew I had to tell my mom. She was the one person who would have embraced me, but I couldn't face her. I told her over the phone and she told my dad, whose reaction I never knew. It was scary, I didn't know where to turn first. If it had been my mother's decision, I suspect now that she would have raised our baby, but my father would never have considered it.

James wanted to get married, but he was still in high school! His father was very wise in handling the situation. When I was at his house, he sat me down and began asking questions: "Do you want to get married?"

"Yeah."

"You know James has to finish school. Do you have a job?"

I did, as a clerk, but I wasn't making enough to support anyone, barely myself. By then I was crying. James' father pointed out, "James can't support you and you can't support a baby. What is left?"

My mother suggested we talk to a social worker at an adoption agency. She was helpful but I wasn't very nice, was pretty sullen. I didn't want to be probed or bothered with questions. She looked like a spinster to me! After three interviews she arranged for me to go to a home in another city. My mother took me there, was very supportive, but it was a lonely, painful time. I cried myself to sleep every night.

It was a boardinghouse, across the street from the hospital where I had to work to pay the rent. The landlady was weird, not very friendly and everyday I walked across the street to a dingy old storeroom in the back recesses of the hospital. It was dark and gloomy there too, which didn't help my mood! I felt very alone. My mom brought my sewing machine to me so I could make maternity clothes. Basically, the family kept it secret. A couple of times I talked to James on the phone and some so-called girlfriends came once, really to see what was going on more than out of concern for me.

After a while another boarder came, Colleen who was an Irish immigrant. She lifted my spirits tremendously as we sat at the kitchen table for long talks. Colleen was older, 27; I was 19. She kept her baby while I felt I had no choice. Once it occurred to me to run away with the baby, but the next question always came: "How will that improve things? How will you take care of this baby?" I had jealousy pangs when I saw Colleen much later with her child.

I wasn't very mature but I would have loved it if my parents said, "We'll help." There was no such offer. I was being pushed and wasn't strong enough to fight. I don't remember a lot of what went on, just being so lonely while everything around me was dreary. When my time came, I was in labor for hours and hours, very painful. I remember holding a nurse's arm during contractions, squeezing my eyes shut and thinking, "Her arm feels like my mother's!" I opened my eyes and there mom was and I felt much better.

After 12 hours my son was born. Because my mom thought it would be easier on me, I didn't ask to see him. During delivery, I was knocked out at the end so I didn't see him then either. Before I left the hospital though, a social worker came to see me, saying that I should see him. "C'mon," she said, "he's right down the hall; let's go have a peek."

The nurse behind the glass held him up, his butt in the palm of her hand, kind of bracing his back with the other hand, making it look like he was sitting up. His eyes were open. I know babies that young can't see, but he was staring straight at me. We were mesmerized—locked. I couldn't take my eyes off of him. Right there I saw myself in him, I saw James in him and I wanted to reach through the glass, pick him up...I had to tear myself away. There's a blank in my memory from there. I don't recall leaving the hospital or talking to anyone, but I certainly must have.

Looking back, I think it was more difficult that I saw the baby. For many nights, years and years, I saw that sweet little face, crying myself to sleep. But if I hadn't, I would have wondered, so I'm glad I got to feast my eyes on him for a little while. No one gave me any information about him, not his weight or length. I remember asking if he was healthy; he wasn't very big, maybe 6 lbs., but they were more interested in asking me about my medical history.

One thing I did get before I left the hospital, which I never told anyone, was a photograph. A little old lady came into my room with the newborn photos, all excited. At first, I thought, "Oh, God, please don't do this to me," and told her, "I'm not supposed to see them." She simply left one for me. I didn't tell my mom, it was so precious to me and helpful to have it.

I don't remember signing final papers—something else I've blocked out. The social worker did tell me she hoped to find a black family for my baby but until then he would be in foster care. Through the years, the hardest part for me was wondering if he was going from foster home to foster home. That was the nightmare I lived, that my baby was unadoptable. Later when I tried to get information from the social worker, she wasn't cooperative at all, told me nothing. It took me 26 years (until my search) to learn that Jed had been placed immediately with a white family.

After leaving the hospital I went to my brother's house to convalesce for two weeks. He was older, married and couldn't have children. I liked his wife too and, during the pregnancy, they wanted to adopt my baby. My mother warned me, "You must think about this very carefully because if you decide the baby stays in our family, you'll have to play the role of an aunt forever."

Thinking I wasn't strong enough to do that, afraid I'd end up going to my brother's and stealing him from his crib, I thought adoption was better. It was a hard decision. With my brother and his wife, I could have seen the baby grow up, but could I keep it secret for years? I was so troubled! I remember my brother sitting in a lounge chair, I crawled onto his lap, crying for my baby and he held me, crying too.

The only other person I could talk to who understood my feelings from the gut was James. During delivery, I was angry at him but it didn't last. Jed was born in 1966 and afterwards, James and I kept seeing each other. My mom knew I was feeling bad, but she, more or less, felt sorry for me while James understood and felt what we had lost—our son. In 1970 we were married, which again did not please both sets of parents. James' grandfather told his father, "Well, you shouldn't be surprised he picked a white woman because you raised him with whites!"

My father wouldn't accept the marriage. I couldn't visit while he was in the house, so mom would come to our house, a small place that James' grandparents gave to us rent-free. I had a job but James had trouble finding one. Eventually it got on my nerves. All day I worked in a hospital scheduling patients for surgery and when I got home, the place was full of our friends who weren't working either. Feeding them dinner too got to be a real drag. Soon I was asking myself, "What's wrong here? I'm the only one working!"

None of our parents mentioned the baby again, but

James talked about finding him, getting him back. Remember we thought that being biracial, he was unadoptable. I didn't want to feel any more pain, not believing James could carry it off anyway, so I told him, "Do whatever you need to do, but don't tell me anything until you can say, 'we're going to pick him up.' "

James did go to the agency, tried to get some information, but again the social worker told him nothing. After we separated, James and I remained friends and eventually he moved to California, got married and had three children. Through the years we stayed in contact. When I began searching for Jed, James was pleased, wanting to know every detail. Every time I saw biracial children in public, I'd look, wondering...is the age right? Could it be? All the time Jed was growing up, maybe five miles from where I lived! It's amazing our paths didn't cross!

I continued working at the hospital, stayed single and acted like I wasn't particularly interested in kids or being a parent. My mother died in 1983 and I miss her terribly, wish she could have been here for my reunion with Jed. She would have loved seeing him too. On the other hand, my father is difficult to understand. He's accepted my second husband who is black, likes him a lot but still does not want to see any pictures of Jed or meet with him. Everyone else in the family is excited, happy for us.

In letters I explained to Jed what the situation was like for James and me at his birth and he accepted it. He seems to want to focus on now, not the past. His adoptive family has been wonderful, very sharing, and I know they gave him a much better life than I could have. When I talk with Jed's mother, I am careful to say "your son" because Jed is their son. She raised him. I told her, "I love your son." When I introduced Jed to my family members, I said "my son" after asking Jed if that was O.K. He has no problem with it.

One thing was nice at Jed's meeting with James' parents: James' father told him, "I want to clear up one point right away. Don't hold a grudge towards Becky or James because giving you up wasn't their fault, wasn't their decision. We four parents made them do it, it was our decision. You should know that."

Having Jed in my life now is the most wonderful, beautiful gift. I am so proud of him. A woman considering adoption today has many choices that I did not have, which is good but—still if I could have found a way at 19 to raise my son, I would have been a mom. My perspective is different now that I know Jed. I look at young children, thinking of all I missed out on. That is sad. Jed has changed my whole life for the better. When he learned about my cancer, he told my husband, "I've only known Becky a short while but I love her already."

Many of Jed's verbal expressions are exactly like James'—a way they both have of saying, "oh boy!" Seeing him, knowing him, touching him—these are the best parts and I feel very hopeful about the future.

LISA

"I know my son is in a good place. He will always know I love him and he will always be loved by those around him. I believe that someday I will be able to stand next to him and love him without distance in between."

The eldest of four children, Lisa had just graduated from a prestigious university when her relationship with Tom resulted in pregnancy. A slender, intense young woman, Lisa explored the adoption process from an intellectual viewpoint, trying to prepare herself also for the emotional consequences. She and the baby's birthfather earnestly "interviewed" staff at two agencies and considered a private placement through an attorney, making it clear that they intended to be actively involved in selecting a family for their child and that they would want information regarding the child's welfare beyond placement for years to come.

Currently Lisa is employed in Philadelphia, attends forums and support groups regarding adoption and is surprised to discover how much more contact she has with her birthson's adoptive family than the other women who have chosen adoption. While Lisa does not have an open adoption, her birthson's parents regard her as part of themselves and hope one day she will choose to meet with them in person.

ꝭ

I believe in the strength of love which makes adoption possible. I am proud to be a birthmother and to have given my son life.

My son was born beautiful. He is growing up physically strong and mentally sharp. I chose for him to be raised by parents I have never met. That he is not with me at times is excruciating; there are moments I feel our separation like a fist in my heart. But there are also times I know that his adoption has given us both a chance to grow up and to take on our world.

I became pregnant when I was 21 years old and a senior in college. Tim and I had been dating for a year and our relationship fluctuated between being very strong and very unfulfilling. Most of the time I wanted to give our relationship all my energy, but there were times I wondered if it was worth it. Our futures seemed as if they would send us on diverging tracks. My plan was to teach English in a rural school in Kenya, and Tim wanted to put his training as an electrical engineer to work. I think sex was our attempt to feel closer.

Tim's intuition told him I was pregnant. I took a home test which showed positive, then verified the results at a local clinic. I panicked, left the clinic crying hysterically, wandered into a parking lot, sat on the asphalt and cried until I couldn't breathe. Tim stood over me watching. We were both terrified and didn't know what to do so we started to walk. We walked around the city for hours discussing our choices, both of us feeling the need to make an immediate decision. We were to graduate in a few weeks, our parents would be in town, and we thought we'd be leaving each other, maybe for good.

I felt as if my body had been invaded; I was angry and despised being pregnant. I even wished for a miscarriage. Tim and I desperately wanted a quick solution, but we could not fit abortion into our ethics. We never discussed marriage. We discussed single-parenting briefly; Tim was clearly not interested in being a single parent, and I was mostly unwilling to take my life in that direction. Adoption was our best choice.

Telling friends helped make my pregnancy more real. I asked one friend to say "you are pregnant" over and over and over. Tim and I were overwhelmed, but we acted quickly. Over the course of a few days we visited a doctor, an abortion clinic (just to be sure of our decision) and an adoption center. I talked with one of my professors, whose calmness was reassuring. And we continued in our studies. It was the week of finals and we wanted desperately to finish our courses.

Tim and I decided to remain in the city after graduation for we were comfortable with the area and we knew we could help each other through the pregnancy. Our greatest fear was telling our parents who lived in other states.

I was raised in a Catholic household. We rarely discussed sex, but I know my parents believe it belongs only in marriage. My mother guessed I was pregnant. She could see it in my face. My parents were supportive of my decision not to abort, but felt betrayed by my decision for adoption. My parents, two sisters and brother tried to be supportive, but they were very hurt, and I think they were relieved that I would not be home during my pregnancy; they did not want to become attached to the child, and then have to say goodbye to a member of the family.

It is my understanding that to this day my parents have not told their friends. When I was five months pregnant, I wanted to come home for my father's 50th birthday celebration. My parents asked that I not come; they did not know how they would answer questions if the guests saw that I was pregnant. My father, my two aunts and my grandparents have still never talked with me about my son. I think they are afraid to upset me with questions or conversation. Maybe they think I have forgotten and they don't want to remind me, or maybe they are trying to forget.

I had a very easy pregnancy and I kept busy with two jobs, spending my free time with Tim and our friends who were still in the area. One of our friends was also pregnant, though she had decided to raise her child. Another friend was raising a daughter she had intended, until her birth, to place for adoption. Tim and I felt sure of adoption. We made all our decisions together, and Tim took an active role as birthfather. I expected nothing less, and Tim never thought of leaving me to fend for myself. He is unusual in this way, and I respect his attention to and care for both me and our child.

I started thinking of the fetus as a child the first time I felt his butterfly kicks. I was lying on my stomach, about four months pregnant, and I could actually feel the baby flutter. I was amazed. Throughout my pregnancy, I was fascinated by my changing body. What was most remarkable to me was how little I had to consciously do. My body took care of itself, it stretched and transformed and readjusted while I took vitamins and watched like a spectator.

I also began to love my baby. I began to talk to him, share how scared I was, point out the wonderful parts of the world, ask him to understand. At the same time, I began to have doubts about adoption. The more I felt him grow inside my womb, the more I loved him. I wanted to stay pregnant forever so that I would never have to say goodbye. But when I would waver, Tim and I would reassess our reasons for adoption, and we always came back to being sure.

It is hard for me to articulate our reasons for adoption. Mostly I think we felt unprepared to be parents, and since we were not going to stay together, were even more overwhelmed by the prospect of parenting alone. We also felt our child needed the security of two parents who were committed to each other, and who could provide not just emotionally and spiritually but financially as well. Tim and I have strong family values and we could not justify pretending to be a family when we were not. We felt young and scared. We felt suffocated by the idea of parenting a child before we had made our marks in the world, achieved our own goals. And we were fiercely independent. Tim's parents offered to help raise our child and I know my parents would have cared for him as well. But Tim and I agreed that we would not be part-time parents, and that if we could not care for him ourselves, we would place him for adoption.

We had been working with an adoption counselor at a private agency since I was about four months pregnant. At first Tim and I just talked with her, and then gradually we began making decisions about adoptive parents. I was furious that the files of adoptive parents only contained letters from adoptive-mothers-to-be. I refused to place my child in a home where the father did not take an active part in the process. Our counselor asked the men to also write their feelings about parenting, and we considered only the couples who obliged. There were few couples we seriously considered. Tim and I each have firm beliefs about how a child should be raised, and we quickly dismissed the homes which seemed too controlling or uncreative or unaffectionate. We were beginning to worry that we would not find a couple whose sense of family matched our own.

I trust my instincts and throughout my pregnancy my instincts were what I most heavily relied upon. My head and my heart were in constant battle so I had to trust my gut. I was immediately attracted to Linda and Jay as prospective parents. Tim and I never met them, but we liked their words. They said they would raise a child to be honest and to know how to love. They wanted to teach their child about the outdoors and about God. They were not threatened by including the birthparents in their child's life—but only on their child's terms. They trusted themselves to be good parents and made no pretenses of being perfect. The bottom line was they wanted a child, they wanted to be a family.

I have since learned to trust Linda's instincts the way I trust my own. I gave birth to my son December 22. The days preceeding Christmas, Linda told her husband she felt they would soon have a baby. Christmas came and went and she started to doubt her intuitions. Had I not wavered about whether to place my son for adoption, Linda and Jay would have met their son on Christmas. Linda knew when her son had been born.

But I did waver. When I held my son for the first time, saw his face, his hands, his feet, his breathing chest, I was ready to change the world for him. I could have held him forever. I was as proud as any mother. He smelled right, felt right, fit my arms perfectly. Tim beamed with pride, looking at his son with love I had never, and have never since, seen in him.

I had been adamantly opposed to foster care because I wanted my child to go directly from the hospital to his new home. But foster care allowed us time to think, so I left the hospital and my son went to temporary care. I cooked Christmas dinner. I went through the motions, but I felt hollow. I was sure I would die if I didn't have my son with me, though I didn't know how to change my life so we could be together. I even began to doubt whether I could trust someone else to raise him. I was completely unprepared for these feelings. Seeing my son's face had changed everything.

I didn't know what to do, and I didn't know where to turn. I was torn. It seemed to me that my adoption counselor wanted me to follow through with adoption. Tim wanted the same. I had another counselor who was out of town for Christmas. My doctor gave me formula to bring home for my baby. Tim's and my family hoped I would raise my son. My friends were reluctant to guide me.

Tim and I signed the adoption papers on the last day of December. I don't remember how I finally made the decision. I don't know how I was able to move the pen. I remember little of that day, only that signing the papers felt like the most violent act of my life. Afterward, I must have stayed in bed for a week. I was too depressed to move, and I was physically trying to recover. My breasts kept producing milk; my body wanted my son.

After my son was born I didn't smile for months. I needed time to grieve but felt guilty for mourning since my son's adoption was my own decision. I moved back home where I did not feel free to talk about my son. Tim was too far away to offer the support I needed. I felt completely abandoned and simultaneously I felt pressure to appear outwardly strong.

But I was devastated. All that winter I fantasized that my son was with me. Sometimes the images were so vivid I thought I was going mad. But when I'd stop myself in the middle of a fantasy, my feelings of aloneness were too much for me to handle. For months I had to fight the urge to physically harm myself. I didn't want to end my life but I wanted a drastic change. I wanted to transfer my emotional pain into concrete, physical pain. I wanted pain I could understand and control. I wanted to heal. Finally spring came and I began to feel more hope, less guilt.

Guilt is a powerful emotion. Until very recently I denied having any guilt feelings and was not able to admit that I chose adoption as much for myself and Tim as for my son. To me that sounded selfish and cruel. But the reality is that adoption did give each of us the best chance to grow. Now I try to focus on the fact that my son is living, that he is loved by so many people, and that Tim and I were a part of the miracle of bringing someone into the world. Though our separation will certainly bring each of us sadness, I hold on to the belief that for all of us there can be mostly joy.

What I want most for my son is for him not to need me. I want him to have a secure place in his family and to feel that Linda is his mother and Jay is his father. I pray that I will someday know him face to face, but I hope that when he chooses to meet me, it is not because I have left him with an aching void. I hope his parents will be able to teach him that my love for him is real and strong, and that it is because of my love and my belief in our timeless connection that I was able to let him go.

I cannot say I would make the same decision again. I cannot go back and second-guess my choice for adoption. I have been constantly evolving as a person, and it is unreasonable to try to remake a decision that was made at a different time, a different place. I can say, however, that if I were to find myself unexpectedly pregnant a second time, I would not choose adoption, because I would not be strong enough to endure the pain twice. But at the time, any of our options would have been difficult and any of our options could have been good. We had to choose. As I see it, the point is not whether we did the singularly right thing, but whether we have been able to subsequently make the decision a good one for us.

It has not been easy. For the first three years I tried to justify my decision by living a lifestyle unconducive to raising a child; I moved from job to job, city to city. I spent six months in Africa and it was there I started to feel more whole; it is true that pain dilutes with time. Meanwhile, I kept in touch with Linda and Jay and our son Mark on a regular basis. I have always tried to be positive in our correspondences because I know that one day Mark will read my letters, and I want him to feel my love and my pride in him and in how he has created a family.

Receiving letters and pictures from Linda kept me going in the first years of Mark's adoption. Linda told me stories and details so that I could picture Mark's new life, and she never forgot to tell me how happy they are, how much they love their son. I believe in them as parents and I know they will help Mark make sense of his place within their home.

Tim and I have maintained mutual friendship, love and respect. He misses Mark, carries his picture in his wallet. I am more protective of myself; my pictures are kept away and I have chosen not to meet Linda and Jay, not to know their last name or where they live. I need this distance. I have also been struggling with how much contact to have with their family. I do not want to be a confusing presence in Mark's life as he grows older. Linda and I are keeping open communications, and taking it year by year.

New issues continuously arise. It is difficult for me to know who to tell about being a birthmother. It is important to make adoption better understood and more readily accepted as an option, but at the same time my son's adoption is highly personal and I am unwilling to open myself to everybody. It is very disappointing to find that adoption is generally misunderstood, and that birthparents are kept on the periphery of most discussions. The stereotype that birthparents are cold-hearted still persists. Even for some of my friends, the choice for adoption is nearly inconceivable.

I am very fortunate, though, to have met a friend who has touched me deeply and has helped me strengthen my positive perspective on adoption. Kent is adopted and is currently searching for his birthparents. He wants to meet his birthparents so that he can thank them. Kent is a warm, open person and has helped me to trust that my son will not feel anger toward me and Tim. Kent's kindness and affirmation of my decision has been, many times, my main support. I have also added an important dimension to his thinking: Kent had no idea that his birthparents are remembering his birthday, picturing him growing older, missing him, keeping him in their prayers. I truly believe that they are.

I love my son. He grew in me, then separated himself from my body at his birth. He is his own person with his own thoughts and dreams and his own natural inclinations. I cannot imagine this world without him. I feel blessed to have given him life.

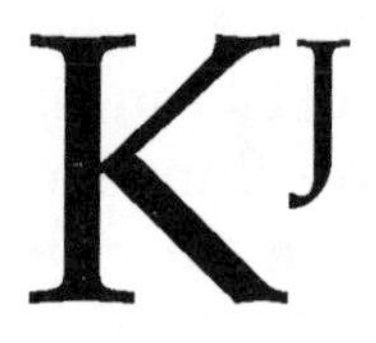

"I couldn't see myself married to him because he couldn't handle everyday responsibilities, so how could he handle the responsibilities for a wife and a child? I still do not regret my decision and I am sure my baby girl is loved..."

Born in 1960 K.J. was the fifth of seven children. She describes herself as a quiet, shy child who was an average student. Her family went to church together regularly and stressed the importance of education. All but one of K.J.'s siblings went to college. During high school, she did not date, then as a 19-year-old college freshman, K.J. met Richard by whom she became pregnant. Realizing the extent of Richard's drinking, K.J. made the decision to end their relationship without telling him of the pregnancy.

When K.J. married at the age of 21, she and her husband, Jim, expected to have several children. After five years of infertility work, including surgery and fertility drugs, the couple went on an adoption waiting list. Four years later a baby girl was placed with them, followed a year and a half later by another baby girl. The couple sends photos and letters regularly to their daughters' birthmothers and has developed a relationship that includes each birthmother visiting their home and being part of the family's life.

ꕥ

Gosh, I can't remember how I met him; it was that long ago and I block it all out too, you know. I'm sure I met him at college at the state university, probably at a party or a friend's. I don't think we had any classes together. I was a freshman. He was pre-med supposedly, but he just kind of goofed off. We started dating in the spring and through the summer. I got pregnant in July but didn't really know it. I ended up breaking up with him shortly after I found out about the pregnancy. He never knew about it.

He was an alcoholic and basically what we did revolved around drinking. We would go somewhere together and he would get drunk and leave me places.

At the time I was living at home with my mom and dad who really loved him. I think part of it was because he was pre-med, but they liked him better than any of the boyfriends that I ever had. He was very good looking also and kind of the life of any party. I met his mom and dad, too.

I wasn't using any sort of birth control, thinking, I guess, that it couldn't happen to me. I guess I was stupid, but he was my first big love. When I did break up with him, he couldn't accept it. He would sit outside my house all night in his car and I just knew that if I told him I was pregnant, he would never leave me alone. I would have never heard the end of it.

Abortion was never a consideration. I think it's a woman's choice, but I couldn't do it.

My parents were real supportive. They were behind me in whatever I chose to do. They stood by my decision to put the baby up for adoption. They knew it was a hard decision and they didn't try to change my mind or influence me or anything. If I had decided to keep it, that would have been all right too.

I didn't really show until the seventh month; then I just didn't go out or anything. The first four months, I didn't see a doctor, then I went to a free clinic. I also got on the W.I.C. Program, but I knew I didn't want to raise the baby by myself. I knew I couldn't provide a good home; I was only making $50 a week. I was trying to go to school and not being married...I think a child should have two parents. I knew I couldn't provide the kind of home I wanted to—even with all my family beside me. By the end of the pregnancy, all my brothers and sisters knew—either they didn't say anything or they let me know that they were being supportive. I didn't have anyone tell me I was horrible or anything like that or disapprove of me. Things were a lot different than they are now—like the agency I went to, it seems my caseworker almost sat in judgment of me. I only met her twice—during my pregnancy to talk about adoption, giving the baby up for adoption—then when I went in to sign the final papers. She didn't present any options to me or help money-wise, which I could have used. It took four years to pay back the loan I took out for the hospital bill.

I wrote a letter and sent a gift to the baby when she was born and I don't know if she ever even got it. I took it down when I signed the final papers. The caseworker never let me know if she delivered it or anything.

If anybody should have been supportive, I think it should have been the agency whereas all my friends and family were supportive of me and they weren't. At least that's how I felt.

I was in the hospital for three days. I held her and fed her and everything. I was feeling tired. For three days, mostly I remember crying. I named her Angela; she looked just like her birthfather, pretty blue eyes and blond hair. For a long time I was emotionally numb.

My parents didn't come to see me in the hospital, I think they just didn't want to see her. Even now I can remember what Angela looked like. I didn't really want any photos then, but I think it would have been nice to have heard from the adoptive parents, maybe during the first year, just to let me know that the baby was O.K.; what her personality was like and if she was a happy baby. I don't know if I would have gone through an open adoption or not. I don't think I would have really been interested at that time, but I would have liked to receive some kind of word. She's 11 years old now.

There was one nurse in the hospital who was great,

really helpful. She was in the labor room with me, talked to me and told me she had given her baby up for adoption, so she really knew what I was going through. She helped me with my feelings.

Afterwards I didn't date at all for a year. I was more careful of who I would go out with and I wouldn't have sex at all. I didn't until I met my husband, Jim. First thing, I told him about the baby. He was great; he just held me and conforted me, didn't ask any questions or be judgmental. He's seven years older than I am. Compared to the other guys I knew or had dated, he was unusual. He had a real job, was mature, instead of being a student.

One thing was very strange. When Jim and I got married, the baby's father heard about it. He sent me a dozen roses and put a big ad in the paper, "Please come back to me." He knew I was getting married. I was just surprised that he didn't show up at my wedding. Thank God he didn't.

When Jim and I found out I was infertile, he brought up one time—"What if you had kept the baby"...but that was the past. That's how I felt; it was behind me. When we were ready to adopt, I told my mom—"Well, I put my baby up for adoption. I know how it feels."

My sisters have asked me if I would want to see my baby now. If she came looking for me, I wouldn't turn her away. I'd accept her, see her, everything...I'd want her to be part of my life, but I think that's up to her right now. I don't think that's my right. It's more her right if she chooses.

One thing I would want to say to her, my baby...is that I hope I did the right thing. I hope she is having a happy childhood, a happy life and that it's happier than it could have been with me. Because I don't know if I would've ended up here, happily married with two daughters, if I would have kept her.

TAMI

"Please don't look down on us for the presents we give our baby. I know they are cheap but we are trying..."

Quickly and without emotion, Tami relates her adoption experience. Her son, Ryan, was born in 1991 when Tami was 19 years old. She was already parenting a one-year-old who is a full sibling to Ryan and living with the boys' father, Julius.

"He doesn't believe in marriage," Tami states, though she is also not certain she wants marriage, "because then I'd be stuck forever and Julius had a bad temper." Recently Tami graduated from high school, which she is very proud of, hoping to attend classes for training as a licensed practical nurse. For now, however, finances are tight and Tami cannot find day care she can afford for her first born.

Tami is unhappy that Julius does not share her joy when she receives pictures and letters from Ryan's adoptive parents. Since she told no one in her family about her second pregnancy and adoption decision, Tami feels very alone dealing with her grief. Contact with her caseworker is ongoing though Tami refuses to attend a support group for birthmothers. Intensifying her aloneness is the fact that Tami is white, Julius is black.

"His family looks down on me and says it isn't right, our relationship, and my family looks down on me because I care about him. I can't win," says Tami. "We've been through so much together since I was 16—two pregnancies...actually three; one had to be aborted on my doctor's advice. I try to be a good parent, but Julius says our son is 'too white'; like I said, I can't win."

I recently had a son that I named Ryan. We put him up for adoption. We already had one son, and couldn't afford another one. We loved him very much. But it just couldn't be.

We already had the plans of giving him up for adoption. So when he was born, I should've never held him. It was a very stressful time for me and his father.

I went through labor alone. The reason being is because nobody knew about the pregnancy.

Neither of our parents knew. It was very difficult. When I was around them, I tried my hardest to hold my belly in. Actually it was easy since I was still big from my other baby. To this day, nobody still don't know. That's the deepest, darkest shadow in my life.

I couldn't tell them, because I was afraid of disappointing them. One day I know I will tell them. Till that day, I will feel a terrible hurt.

Don't get me wrong, I loved my baby and still do, and always will.

I hope to meet him when he's older.

I know I did what was best for him.

CATHLEEN

"When I met my oldest birthdaughter, it was like looking at myself in a mirror."

Cathleen was born in 1941. She is the mother of three grown children whom she raised as a single parent after divorcing their father. She is also the birthmother of three daughters, born in 1965, 1968 and 1970. Although she speaks willingly, and on the surface easily, Carol was surprised, speechless and tearful when she learned that her eldest birthdaughter was interested in making contact with her.

❧

There were four of us, growing up. My dad actually raised us after my mom passed away. I was eight and the oldest. A year after my mom died, my dad married again and we moved into the country, going to Catholic schools. I liked my stepmother; my dad was a house painter. When we would be off for the summer, a lot of times my dad would have us come to work with him and we would watch him paint. Other times we would stay at home. I was kind of the head of the household while he was gone. We had chores to do, the dishes and the laundry and ironing, and that was more mine than the other kids because I was the oldest, but they still did their part.

My dad would bring fresh meat home everyday. Living out in the country, we had neighbors that brought us corn and vegetables and stuff from their gardens so that was nice. I really enjoyed my childhood. We always had hand-me-down clothes. That's the one thing I wished we would have been able to have had—better clothes—but they were still nice, you know, they were just not new to us.

I don't think I really dated until my senior year in high school. I don't even remember who was my first date; I do know that out of high school I got myself a job working in a "5 and 10"-type store and started dating the man who was my first husband. I liked him right away—when I saw him, I said "That's the guy I'm going to marry." And I did, but it didn't turn out real great. In the meantime we had three kids. We started off right away because I was pregnant before we got married and we just had them one after another. I think at the farthest they were only 12 months apart so they were right up on each other. I got married at the age of 20. I thought it was automatically part of life and never really tried to protect myself or do any type of birth control methods; they just came, the kids…

I feel we were both really young. I know that I was real naive, so it had a lot to do with that. He was not Catholic, but he signed papers so the kids could be raised Catholic. After we broke up, he started seeing someone else, a cousin's wife. He ended up marrying her, still is married to her so I guess there was something there!

I would say there have always been men in my life; it seems like they were always just there. At one time I know I felt, "Golly, maybe if I gained weight I wouldn't have such a problem. Maybe they would leave me alone." I guess I meant sex-wise more than just being around because I like to have somebody around. I enjoy the company and dating. I'd say, I don't know, they just always seemed to be there!

I was dating two guys; now I'm really not certain who was the father. You see I was living with another girl, we were able to date and go out at night and I used to go out dancing and I would meet people on the dance floor. It was like the one guy, of course, I knew;

I had known him for years. I was just meeting him again and he's been in my life ever since, you know, he's just there. The other one was someone I had met on the dance floor, then we dated; he came to my home. He was really good with the kids; he would bring them ice cream and we would go out and he seemed like a really nice guy. I seen him a couple of times since, I don't think he is as nice as I thought he was then. Maybe I've changed, maybe he has changed.

They were both in their 20s, one single, but the one I had just met was not single. I knew the other one had been married because I'd seen part of his wedding party. He had gotten married on a bike and they had a motor or bike cavalcade, I guess you would call it. In those days he was a pretty wild type character and, of course, when I first met him, he scared me to death, but he was a kind type person. He wasn't forceful; he wasn't the kind of person who would actually slip something to you in a drink, and I was really lucky; I could have got caught into something I really didn't like or couldn't handle.

I think I thought about asking for money for an abortion, but then I never did; it's funny, I just thought I would go right ahead and have the baby rather than ask for money. Meanwhile my roommate's husband came back home to her, so I moved out to my dad's with three kids. He had fixed the basement up with paneling. The four of us lived down in the basement...I guess we kind of settled in. We were allowed to use the rest of the house, of course, and I would help him with the dinners and the dishes and such and my sister, my youngest sister, was still living at home.

I would talk to a friend of mine who was a priest about different options and I chose adoption. I wanted to make sure the baby was O.K. before I signed any papers, so I wanted to hold her. I felt I was entitled to do that. A friend of mine, Melanie, just happened to be in the hospital when I was getting ready to deliver; she and I were walking around together (she was going to deliver too) so I named the baby after her.

The second baby's father was someone I had known for a while, even before Melanie was born. I must have bumped into him, I guess that's how it happened. I bumped into him again one night and that was it. No birth control, I just didn't even think about it. Like I said I was real naive and felt that—you know—life is life and you're suposed to just keep on and I never thought about birth control. I know in between Melanie being born and the second one, I had hepatitis. My sister had come home and she had been very sick and just using the same glass in the kitchen by the sink. I ended up getting hepatitis. I was just getting over it when I went out, this was the first guy that—you know—that I had been with since Melanie's birth.

I was still living with my dad, taking care of my sister's kids and my three, getting them into school and everything. I don't even remember thinking about keeping the baby and I don't know why I didn't even think about it. The father was single and I told him about the pregnancy—actually he was a little bit of a drinker and he was a full-blooded Indian. I knew he drank a bit—but he was kind of a—well—I kind of liked him. He was a nice enough guy.

I went to the same agency. I wouldn't say I went to counseling, because I really enjoyed my caseworker, just talking to her. She was a real nice person. I would bump into her here and there after the children were adopted and she would ask me about my family and we would talk. I trusted her and the agency to do the right thing for my babies.

The second little girl I named Tina because I really

liked the name. The second time I knew what was going to happen. I went to the hospital alone; my dad would never go into a hospital, but he was real good about calling me up on the phone to talk with me. Everyone at the hospital treated me fine; it was something I had to do all by myself, and my dad had to take care of my other kids too.

I knew the adoptive family wouldn't keep her name, Tina...there was a deep emotion there, you know, when you hold the baby and know it's the last time. I saw her in the hospital nursery and I saw her when I signed the papers. I got photos of her too, but when I got home, I hid them so they would not be popping up where the kids would have them. I have photos of all three fathers too.

I felt adoption was the right thing in my case to do but that doesn't necessarily mean it would be right in every case. It is a hard choice to make—it really is—but I felt in my case that the family would be right—would be able to raise them much better because I just didn't have the funds. I wasn't working in the beginning and there was no way I could possibly provide for the babies. I've always known that family life was important and I've always thought that two parents is the way children should be raised.

Booze was not involved. I always knew what I was doing. I had no excuse. The third time, Hank was the father. I thought he was single, but I found out later he wasn't. He had a family, but he paid the bill for this baby. I paid for the others. I wasn't mad I was pregnant, but, in the hospital, I just cried and cried. They had somebody there to watch me every minute and they were afraid I was going to do something and I had nothing in my mind to do, you know, they just had that feeling. They moved me way into a different section; I think that because of the gas that they gave me. I just could not stop crying. I think I cried forever! They wouldn't let me see this baby and I couldn't understand that so I thought Hank somehow arranged it because he did have an important job. It did seem like some sort of arrangement had been made. I think they all thought I would try to take the baby out of the hospital. I left the hospital crying—alone.

When I went to the agency to sign the papers, I remember giving the baby a blanket—a little silky type thing with a pillow and I gave her the name Margo. I was almost 30 at this time; my three kids were still at my dad's 'cause that was my only permanent place. I felt if I ever left my dad's, I'd never have another home and with three kids, I wasn't about to do that.

My caseworker said to me, "I know you love kids, but we have got to do something here." She felt it was important that maybe I think about doing something since I seemed to be very fertile, so I looked into getting some pills which I had for a while. Then they put me on the coil, but I had a lot of pain so I was scheduled to have Band-Aid surgery. Something happened during it and later I had a hysterectomy.

After Margo's birth, I did decide to live on my own. My dad purchased a house in town and moved me in. The bus route was right there and the house my grandmother lived in was just down the street. My kids were now in school full-time and I was on welfare. Then they said to me, "Come on now, we have to get you a job." I loved to sew so they started me off at sewing. I was really a lucky person because I was also getting child support from my kids' father. Once he skipped and was put in jail, but after that he kept his same job and the money came automatically. I also did sewing at different times in my own home—they would bring me the material. After a while I started working two jobs part-time—one in a drug store and one in a laundromat, which I liked.

Different men I had known came back into my life. I didn't know why, they just seemed to come. You would think I would have found somebody permanent. I ended up marrying Ed and that was just before my hysterectomy. He was older and I didn't expect to have any children by him. He had his family and I had mine. By then my kids were older. I had been divorced 17 years.

Ed moved into my home and I ended up keeping the same bills—paying all the bills I was paying before. We did use his money to go on trips and things. I always felt like he had money in his pocket and I never had any. He would eat out at lunchtime and I would have to bring my lunch to work—you know—I felt bad about it. There should have been a different way of being able to solve the problem because there were a lot of times when we really had a good time. I think of the three years I was married to him, we lived together maybe two. He ended up leaving me one time and started drinking again. He had been an alcoholic and had done without for 12 years. Then he started seeing another woman, drinking and all—ended up in the hospital. They said he could only have one visitor—he chose me and we ended up back together for a while. Only the other woman was always around, kind of pulling at him. One day, he left me, going with her.

My three kids are great. Two boys and a girl. They knew about Melanie, Margo and Tina because I put their names on a calendar by their birthdays and their ages. I always did that and when I knew they were over 18 years old, I went back to the agency to search for them. Melanie had already gotten in touch with them. She was 25 the year I began the search. It was strange because before I went to the agency I woke up one morning and said to my daughter, "Somebody was calling me and I thought it was you, but it wasn't your voice." She said it wasn't her and I began to think it was Melanie calling me. I have had a lot of things like that happen to me throughout my life, so I don't always pay a lot of attention.

I wrote three letters—one each to Tina, Margo and Melanie and since Melanie had already asked the agency...she got her letter. I talked to a caseworker several times and so did Melanie before we got to meet. Of course, her name is not Melanie any longer because her adoptive parents named her Cindy. When we met, it was wonderful...I went to Cindy's wedding and her family told me how she was as a child, that she had been a really nice child, never got in any trouble. She was very friendly and everybody always liked her, just a real nice girl. Her parents were divorced. I felt sad about that because I wanted her to have a family together all those years and she didn't. Cindy looks a lot like me, she really does; same eyes...I can see myself in the way she twists and turns, the way I was as a teenager. Her adoptive mom was very nice too. Cindy asked about her birthfather; she wants to know about him too. I had to tell her I wasn't sure...which one of two was her father.

A year later I got to meet Margo—she has a different name too. Her adoptive family had contacted the agency because she always said, "I want my birthmother to be at my wedding." We found each other in time.

Now I have to find Tina. Someday I believe it will happen. I have no regrets. My kids are beautiful people.

KRISTEN

"Seeing you for the first time, I loved you instantly, but I knew that you were not mine but were another couple's child, a couple who had been waiting for you a long time."

Kristen is a tall redhead, the youngest of five children. After the initial shock of learning of their daughter's pregnancy, Kristen's parents took an active part in the counseling process which began in Kristen's second month. While vacillating between her original choice of adoption versus parenting, Kristen attended an agency-sponsored adoption education group for prospective parents. Listening to the hopes of these couples for parenthood helped her immensely.

Saying goodbye to her newborn son in intensive care was the hardest day of Kristen's life. The couple she selected met with her one time prior to placement while the baby was in foster care and final papers had not been signed. A month later Kristen entered a restaurant and recognized immediately the adoptive mother carrying her birthson. Quietly and in tears, Kristen turned and backed out the door. Her initial desire was not to embarrass the adoptive family by her presence. Her anguish was in the realization that she no longer would have recognized her birthson.

Kristen returned to college, volunteering at a crisis pregnancy center. She is verbal, outspoken and determined not to be ashamed of her pregnancy or adoption decision. She exchanges one or two letters a year with her adoptive couple through the agency, looking forward to the day she is financially independent of her parents and hopes that someday she'll have "a wonderful marriage and a beautiful child."

❧

I met Michael the summer after I graduated from high school and fell madly in love with him instantly.

Without a doubt, he was my first major love. During high school I had some relationships with guys, but it was mostly just going out with friends, maybe going to a guy's basketball game, which was a lot of fun—no pressure—very easy going...with Michael though it was a heavy, instant fall. I was 19.

Michael was doing construction work. He couldn't stand being cooped up in an office all day and neither could I. After we started dating, we were always together. From friendship, our relationship grew and was a lot of fun. Michael drove a truck, which I loved riding in. He grew up in the country, a different lifestyle than I knew. It was neat, getting to know his friends, how they differed from mine, listening to country music and going places together.

I met Michael's father and his brother. His parents were divorced. He met my parents, who thought we were kind of rushing things because we were always together, but you know that's a natural reaction from parents. They thought he was really shy and couldn't figure out how I got along with him because he didn't talk much, but they saw I was happy. He treated me nice and he always came to get me and he was always on time—at first.

In the fall I went away to college; Michael came to visit me every weekend or I came home. He'd call me two or three times a day sometimes. He's very intelligent, would help me with my math over the phone. His parents are both college graduates, but they didn't seem to encourage their kids to go. At one point, Michael wanted to go, but he had no support from his parents. Or maybe he just said he wanted to go because we were dating at that point. He could have aspired to a lot.

When Michael visited me, my roommate would leave and one thing led to another. I was kind of ignorant, not that I didn't know about sex, but I was a virgin. I knew about birth control, where to get it, but I thought it would take away from the whole excitement of sex. I know that's stupid now.

Then my period was late. I called Michael, kind of upset and said I was a little worried. He brushed me off. "You're just worried about it—that's why you're not getting it." Then I called him when I got the tests back and they were positive. I was crying and I couldn't talk to him because I was too embarrassed.

You see, Michael had gotten a girl pregnant previously—before we met. All I could think was, "It's happened again. Here I go..." He stopped calling as much, wouldn't come to see me at school and I was a wreck. My girlfriend called Michael, had some choice words she gave him, saying he'd better come deal with this. When he did come to the college he was crying, but I don't know if it was over the fact that I was pregnant or that he got another girl pregnant: if he was crying for us—or for himself!

Before I was pregnant—one time Michael and I saw a couple with a kid at a restaurant. The kid was acting up and Michael said, "I don't know why they don't discipline him. When we have our kid, it won't be that way." I was dumb enough to think I had a future with him, but he had no intention of ever staying with me. Our relationship went downhill—at first, I thought it was the stress of the pregnancy and that he was trying to deal with it, but he was only trying to get away from it.

My grades were suffering and I was sick. I decided I couldn't stay at school so I dropped out and went home; I made Michael come with me to tell my parents. Now I don't think that was such a great idea because my mom yelled at Michael and he didn't say anything, just sat there. It made him look bad so I told him to get out and let me talk.

My mom was hysterical, though she didn't cry. She was laughing, like it was some kind of joke. I wanted to hit her, I said, "I don't really think this is funny." My dad just sat there too, which I knew was even worse because I'd rather have him yell than not say anything.

I felt like I was a big embarrassment to them. I know now that's not what they were saying to me, but that's what I felt—this great Christian family, high standing and their daughter screwed up. I believe my parents brought me up right, taught me the difference between right and wrong, but when I was with Michael, none of that was on my mind. That's what I tried to tell them. The pregnancy had no reflection on them as parents.

I know I disappointed my parents and they thought it was a bad situation to be pregnant and unmarried. I realize it's not exactly fun, but I don't think of it as "bad" because I believe it happened for a reason. My belief in God is very strong, personal, and it helped me get through everything. That may sound stupid, but I always knew I was pregnant for a reason. When people found out and remarked, "That's too bad," as though I was about to die or was supposed to walk around depressed, pregnant and in a funk about it, I didn't feel that way at all.

From the very first, I had said to Michael, "I'm not getting an abortion." A lot of his friends had gotten their girlfriends pregnant—they had abortions and I saw it could be an easy solution, but it wasn't for me. I couldn't have lived with it. Adoption was my first decision. I wanted to go back to school and thought there was no way to have a baby and stay in school. I did talk to a lot of girls who kept their babies, sometimes thinking, "I could do this."

My relatives got involved; everybody knew about

the pregnancy, but no one really said, "You should do this or you should do that." They said, "If Kelly keeps the baby…" I felt a little pressure, but it was my decision, what people said to me didn't sway me. I thought that if the baby were a girl, I'd keep it. People gasp when I say that, but I thought a girl would somehow be more emotional finding out she was adopted as opposed to a boy. With a girl, I would feel I was giving myself away—more so than a boy. It didn't mean I would love a boy less, I thought I'd be more attached to a girl.

I talked to my mom about adoption and she too felt she couldn't handle it if I had a girl and placed her for adoption. I think God knew that and that's why I had a boy. Instinctively, I felt from very early that the baby would be a boy. Adoption can't be an emotional decision—it has to be practical too, not only for the baby but for myself and my family, that's what I thought.

I wanted my child to have a father. Something important is missing without a father. I didn't want to ever regret coming home to a baby; ever be depressed or begrudge a child the care it needs. Some of my reasons for adoption were selfish ones: how would I ever be able to date again? My social life would be totally cut down at age 19. Even though my friends said they'd help babysit, I knew that would last a month or two. They'd go back to school, babysitting would get old. It would take me five to six more years to get through college, trying to find babysitters, working and depending on my parents. They were at the age when they should enjoy their own lives, not be taking care of a daughter struggling to make ends meet with a baby. I didn't want to go on welfare—ever.

In the back of my mind too was the thought that a boy would remind me of Michael and that could be a problem. Maybe I'd get over it quick, but was it fair to the baby? I don't know if I'll ever get over the lies Michael told me, that hurt me a lot. Trying to figure out if he had changed his personality 360 degrees or if he was never the person I thought he was. I don't want to make excuses for Michael, but the way he acted while I was pregnant was not the Michael I knew before. That's very hard to understand. The shy, quiet, great guy became a jerk.

I don't even have a picture of me pregnant; now I try not to think of what being pregnant was like because after my son was born, my stomach felt dead. Someday I'd like to have five or six kids—it was fun having someone growing in me, but marriage is the key word. My friends always wanted to touch my stomach, feel the baby move and they would get upset when I said no. I didn't want them to get excited or attached to the baby either. They didn't understand that. I also told them, "Don't plan any showers for me. Don't buy me anything. I don't need any more pressure on myself than I already have."

The pregnancy should have been an exciting time for me, my family and friends. Instead there was a cloud hanging over it, not being able to talk about names for the baby, where he'd go to school—stuff like that.

I named my son Joseph and that's who he'll always be to me, though I also like the name his adoptive parents chose. Joseph had breathing problems and was in intensive care for several days. In a way I felt that was my fault and it made me want to take him home. It sounds terrible, but in an awful way, I kind of hoped something would be wrong with him so the couple wouldn't want him and I would have no choice, I'd have to take him home. What I was really looking for was a decision to be made for me. I didn't truly want anything to be wrong.

In the hospital there was nothing but pain and

emotion. I tried to look strong, be strong so no one could see how upset I really was. The hardest day was leaving the hospital; the nurse took me right past the door to intensive care, that's where the elevators were and I could hear babies crying. I said to myself, "What kind of mother are you, going home?"...I could picture, I could see my son in there crying. I will never have a harder day than that day.

When Joseph was eight days old and in foster care, I chose a family for him by reading letters from couples at the agency. I wanted to meet them before I signed any papers, even though I felt like I was dangling a baby in front of them. It never occurred to me that I wouldn't like John and Molly after I read their letter and the instant I met them, I knew they were the right parents for Joseph. That night I felt very peaceful about adoption.

The only thing I would change is—it would have been nice to have met John and Molly during the pregnancy. I know they would be taking a risk but especially with Molly, there would have been woman things she could be tuned in with. It would have closed the circle. I would have been comfortable handing him to them.

I think John and Molly are great people, I think of them as friends, and if I ever run into them, I would say "hello." I would love to see them all together, how they interact, that everything is O.K., but I don't have an underlying obsession about it or any desire to follow them around or steal Joseph. I would not be upset to hear him calling Molly "mommy." I am glad he has a mommy and a daddy who is always there for him. It makes me happy to think how much pleasure Molly and John have to be Joseph's parents.

When I look at the pictures I've received of Joseph, they do not make me cry, not once. I laugh because he looks so cute, so happy. I'm not ashamed of having been pregnant and unmarried or having chosen adoption. My mom says to me, "Kristen, you don't have to tell everyone." I think if people know how I feel, that when hard things happen, they can be handled, they can be talked about and they can make a person stronger. I don't want people to feel sorry or sad for me because I am proud of Joseph and his family.

My father won't look at Joseph's pictures. He doesn't want to break down, it hurts him too much and he doesn't want me to see him upset. Yet he does volunteer work for a women's center. He can go out and help other girls who are pregnant, keeping their babies, but he can't share in my excitement when I receive a picture of Joseph. Sometimes that makes me mad, but I guess it's the way he needs to handle it.

One of these days it's all going to catch up with Michael and I wouldn't want to be around him when it does. I went to his house, asked him, "Would you like to see pictures of the baby?" He shook his head no and left. That killed me. I try to give him the benefit of doubt, like maybe it hurts him too, maybe he feels guilty, but I don't think so because I know now that he has gotten two other girls pregnant after me! That is sick. I can't even imagine how he can be hurting so many people, the girls, his family—the babies! It is very hard to have nice thoughts about Michael. He apparently doesn't know what good is.

Sometimes I wonder if I get close to the wrong type of people. Now it's hard to open up and I'm more careful; I don't date anyone my own age, only older guys and I'm on birth control. What Michael did to me was harder than the adoption, his not taking responsibility for anything. I've gone back to school and would like to have a career in social work as well as a family someday.

I hope Joseph will look for me when he's older, not

just for a shallow reason like he's curious about what I look like. I think a part of me will be hurt if he didn't try to find me, but if he doesn't, I'm not going to look for him. It will be his decision. If he has so much at home that he's not bitter, doesn't hate me or think I was a bad person, then it will have been the right decision whether he looks for me or not.

CHRIS

"Other girls called me stupid for choosing adoption. Now they are all whining about no money and having to care for their kid."

At age 14, barely a year after her father's death, Chris became pregnant by her first "serious" boyfriend who was 16 years old. When her pregnancy became obvious, she dropped out of school, upset over being called "a slut" by classmates.

Late at night Chris would climb into bed with her mother, able to talk more freely in the darkness. Though she wished at times that she'd "never been born," Chris forced herself to look for a job, finding one in an ice cream store. She purchased clothing for her baby, wanting her "to go with something of her own to her new family."

Two months after Chris delivered, she returned to school, eventually remarking "how good it felt to be a kid again, swimming and having fun." In her senior year of high school now, Chris displays a maturity beyond her age, plans to study for a beautician's license and hopes to earn enough to study nursing eventually.

In a letter to her daughter's adoptive parents, Chris wrote:

> *"I thank you with all my heart for loving her and parenting her...I want her to understand that I love her...and always will...that I didn't take the easy way out. I made one of the hardest decisions of my life."*

ર્

I was always daddy's girl. When I was small, I would stay at a babysitter's while my parents worked. Then at home my mom would do the cooking and take care of my younger brother so it was my dad and me together. He would play with me, take me places. We were really close. From the time I was nine Dad told me, "When you get old enough, I'm going to put you on the pill because I know how some things end up. I'm not telling you to go out and do it, but I want to be open with you."

My mom never talked to me about sex. She put a clamp on it. I tried so many times to bring it up with her, but my mom had only one boyfriend in her life—my dad. They started dating when she was 15 and got married early. They were married 20 years when my dad died. I was 13 then. He had lung cancer and was sick for a year. When he left, it was like my mom and my brother and I didn't have anybody. I had friends, but I didn't have a guy I was close to. I already knew Paul; my dad knew him too, but it wasn't like we were really dating. We talked on the phone—stuff like that—then Paul stopped calling me and I refused to call him.

It was the beginning of my freshmen year. I was getting good grades then. My dad was gone. I think there was a relationship between my getting pregnant and my dad being gone. If he had been alive, I could have been prepared, I wanted to be prepared; I said to my mom, "So and so is going on the birth control pill." Mom told me straight out, "You are never getting on anything like that. I don't care what happens." So I sort of blamed her too.

Then Paul and I started seeing each other, about nine months before I got pregnant. We would go bowling; sometimes we went to his house. I never told my mom that his parents weren't there because then she wouldn't let me go.

I had a feeling I was pregnant. I took a pregnancy test that I bought in a store and I kind of thought to myself, "Well this is not right. They are only so much percent sure." Then I went to Planned Parenthood with a girlfriend and they told me I was pregnant. I had told Paul I thought I was pregnant and was going to find out for sure. He, automatically, the first time I told him, just stopped calling as much and he was always busy with his friends. He finally said he wasn't going to see me anymore and I said, "Well, I'm going to have your baby."

Paul said, "I don't even know it it's mine." He got that kind of attitude. "It could be so-and-so's..." I was really hurt. I cried myself to sleep the whole nine months, every night. At school I cried, my grades dropped to D's. But I didn't feel pregnant. I was never actually sick—just once I was brushing my teeth and the toothbrush in my mouth made me feel sick. That was all. And I could smell peanut butter everywhere I went which was pretty odd.

I didn't cry around my mom and I wasn't showing. Paul wanted an abortion. I was still in love with him and I thought, "Maybe I could do it," and then I'd think, "No, I can't ." I finally told him, "I'm not going to do it," and that's really when it was over. He said, "Fine, we just won't have anything to do with each other anymore," and I said, "That's what you think."

I went to the dean of girls at school and asked her to help me because I didn't know how my mom was going to react. Telling her would be really hard. Meanwhile though, my best friend told her mom who was also a friend to my mom. When my mom came home from work, the phone rang. Her friend said, "Charlene, go hug your daughter," and when we were hugging, she said, "Charlene, your daughter is pregnant."

My mom was angry and sad. She gave me three weeks to tell Paul's parents or on the final day at 6 o'clock she'd tell them herself. I was about four months pregnant then and it was Christmas. The stress of going all that time without telling my mom, it was like as soon as my mom found out, I just grew, all in a week. My jeans were size 5, I could still fit into them; suddenly they wouldn't zip up anymore!

I told Paul about the deadline. On the final day he had his sister tell his mom and dad, "Chris is pregnant and there is a 50-50 chance it's Paul's." When my mom called, she said she believed me. His parents were really happy and embarrassed. They said that if I decided to keep it they would pay support. Paul was really upset with them, almost left the house because of what they said. When Paul's parents found out I was only 14, they decided adoption would be best for me and the baby too.

I reached a point where I was tired of talking about the pregnancy. I felt I was too young to be able to handle a baby. I wanted to finish high school and I felt the baby would be better off with two parents, financially and emotionally better off—instead of me as a mom saying to a kid, "We're not going to eat for two weeks because we have to get winter boots!"

My mom went with me to an adoption agency. I also went to a support group at school for girls who were pregnant, but they were going to keep their babies. My grandma, who had 14 kids, told me that she would give me $100 a month if I kept the baby. She would care for it in the winter and I could have it in the summer. Well, no five-year-old wants to be with an 80-year-old grandma and grandpa all the time! Then my aunt and uncle, who can't have kids—my uncle won't go to an adoption agency—my grandma said, "Give it to them." I couldn't handle that, in the family; it would be too hard. I'd go over there and they would be doing something to her and I'd go, "Wait a minute, I don't like it that way." I wouldn't want to see my baby call somebody else mommy and daddy or them not dressing her right. I'm afraid I'd be doing that or I'd become best buddies with them and be over there all the time.

It wouldn't work. I knew I couldn't handle that.

My caseworker said I could choose a family for my baby. I wanted them to be Christians, to like animals and to have pets. And I wanted the adoptive mom to be home all day until, at least, the child went to school. And I wanted them to be able to adopt other children so mine wouldn't be an only child. I wanted them to like the outdoors, stuff like camping, and I didn't want them to live anywhere near where I did.

In the hospital I was happy, really happy that it was over and that she was here. I got to sleep on my stomach finally too, that was the best part. Paul's parents came up the second day before I went home. They agreed with me, that she had Paul's eyes and I think his mouth. She was very tiny, like Paul's sister, small-boned and very blond, like me. Delivery was hard but I think that the hardest part is leaving the hospital. I think maybe a lot more people would be willing to give their babies up if they could be away from the baby for one week, knowing that they could still have her back. I think that would help out a lot if they could just do that.

My baby was in foster care for two weeks. A lot of people asked me, "How could you do that? How could you just walk away from the hospital?" The way I've thought of it is, "Yes, I did sign a temporary paper, but if I want her back I can get her back." Just like that, you know. Just call up the agency. As long as I knew that I could have her back, then it was all right being without her. My hormones were going nuts. Then everything started to calm down and my life started to get back to normal where I could actually think about it. It would have been harder to make the decision if I had her with me all that time. It was better that I had time to get my thinking cleared up.

There are all these movies where the mother

doesn't even get to hold the baby. The baby is just gone and the rest of their life they wonder where their kid is. I think it's bad when you do adoption that way. I don't want to know the names of my baby's family, their first names would be O.K. I'd like to know how tall they are and an idea of what they look like. I don't actually want to see a picture of them. I kind of want to know more than that, but then again I don't.

Right after I gave her up I had nightmares. Like she would be 18 or 16 and she would find me and tell me how bad of a life she had and how this happened and that happened and her life has been a total disaster. I would feel at fault. Now I know that anybody that is willing to spend that much money and wait that many years for a baby and try that hard, that ain't going to happen.

I wish I could have had her when I was 18. Three years later I could have kept her. I would have had a better chance in the world, like getting a job and getting help, whatever. Fifteen years old and just being with mom! Even with my dad it might have been better, but it was just my mom. I was actually afraid I'd take it out on the baby somehow. She wouldn't have had anything with me.

I told Paul I wasn't going to sign the final papers until he came over to the house and we talked about it, instead of over the phone, having this screaming match, hanging up. I told him he was going to come over and we were going to try to act a little mature about the situation and talk about it. I showed him the pictures from the hospital of the baby and he did admit that he knew she was his. He was scared. He had never been with anybody else and I had never been with anybody else either.

My mom knitted a blanket for my baby. Everybody said she looked exactly like me, so sometimes I have these daydreams: I'm going to come up to this door and open it and there is going to be me—like looking into a mirror—only younger! I'd be happy, sitting and thinking of how some day that will happen.

I wrote her adoptive parents a letter, telling them more about me and why I did it. It's hard. I go to write something down and it is totally blank. "No, I don't want to put it this way. No I don't want to put it that way," or I'd get it written and I'd throw it away. I just want it to be perfect. Now I want to wait a while before I write the letter. I just want to wait. I'm not exactly sure how I want to put it and I have thought about it a lot.

I've talked to a couple of girls who decided not to go through an adoption. They decided to keep their babies and go on welfare. I almost feel sorry for them because I know how their life is going to turn out. A lot of their parents aren't living in a good house or anything. My baby will have a better chance. Having her at 15, I'd just go backwards, struggling all the time. I'd probably never be able to send her to college. Now she has a better chance to go to college. From all the stress, if I raised her, I would have been a grump, like: I don't want to do this—I'd really rather be out with my friends. That's how I'd feel at 15.

A couple of my friends that were pregnant would say, "I don't want to tell my mom and I don't want an abortion, but I think I will have to get one just because of what my parents will say, they might beat me up or something."

I'd say, "No parent is going to beat you up if you are pregnant, not unless they are really crazy and I know your parents aren't like that!" I would say: "If you are really serious about it then go to an adoption agency. The counselors won't force you one way or the other. They will just give you either side of the story, the good points and the bad points."

Some of the girls that I was pregnant with at school, when I went back to school, they said they wished they had done adoption like I did. Their babies were about a year old now. Their parents, the grandparents have custody of them—or else they're the ones who are watching the babies all the time. The mothers hardly have a chance to see them.

Sometimes I'm afraid I won't be able to have another baby—like when I'm married; maybe two or three years after being married, I'd want to have a family. Now I'm dating a guy, Marty—he's three years older than I am. He's already taken me looking for a ring. Now I am on birth control. When I started dating again, it was going to be my way. I made sure the guy had a steady job and was a high school graduate. He couldn't be a drinker. I'd tell each one, the first week or so, I'd drive them with questions. I'd tell them: "I have a baby. I gave her up for adoption. What would you do if you were in that kind of position? Would you run away from it? Would you be willing to help out as much as you can?" They had to have a really nice attitude.

Marty was special, he actually took me out on a date and spent money. It wasn't just going to a friend's house, like other guys. Marty bought me roses and was looking for a serious relationship like I was. He doesn't believe in abortion either. If we get married, I want to wait at least three years before we have a family so I'd know we'd stay together. I want it to be perfect—not just add a little person that we can't do anything for!

I'd want to stay home with my kids, but before that could happen we'd have to be financially set. That's my goal. I've got it set and that's the way it's going to have to be. I don't want to be one of those mothers that gets up at 3 in the morning, gets kids up, gets them dressed and fed and gets to a factory by 5 or 6 A.M. And then have to take them home and not be able to spend any time with them!

What really upset me was that after my baby was born—about six months later my mom got pregnant. She was dating and then she married the baby's father, who is only three years older than my boyfriend, Marty. That is really odd. My stepfather is only six years older than I am. His mother is only a year older than my mom! It's a complete turnaround because when I was pregnant, my mom said, "I've raised my family."

My mom didn't want to have a whole new family and now she's done just that. Now it's not like mother and daughter. It's like two couples. My stepfather and Marty even like the same kind of music. I don't listen to it and neither does my mom, so we just look at each other and leave the room. I don't really think of him as my stepfather—I think of him as my mom's husband.

I did see all the problems my mom had during her pregnancy. She would cry for hours. Now I help care for my little sister and that helps me a little bit. Sometimes I think about what it would have been like if my baby were with me. It would have been two small babies in the same house! I think it is for the better that my baby has a good family who can give her things that she would never have been able to have with me.

I hope her adoptive parents tell her that I had a good heart and that I love her.

DONNA

"I really messed up but my daughter is not a mistake. I believe God made her for a reason."

Born in West Virginia, Donna's marriage took her to the Midwest where she became involved with an older, married man. Her pregnancy almost destroyed her relationship with her husband. Resolutely, Donna began a search for an adoptive placement for her baby that would be totally open.

The ongoing relationship with Don and Pat, the adoptive parents of Jessica, includes Donna as her birthmother. She visits Jessica several times a year, somewhat to the dismay of extended family members on both sides. Feeling Jessica and her adoptive family are and always will be part of her life too, Donna is actively learning more about open adoption. She attends a birthmother's support group regularly, often feeling bad that her adoption "is so wonderful" compared to the closed and semi-open adoptions of the other women.

Donna's husband does not take part in her relationship with Don, Pat and Jessica nor does the biological father, Mitchell. Since Donna suffers from endometriosis, she is particularly worried about her ability to carry another child to term. A year and a half after Jessica's birth, Donna's second pregnancy, by her husband, resulted in a miscarriage.

ɕ

I'm the youngest of six kids and I was raised in a Catholic home. I have four brothers and a sister. My parents were divorced when I was 12, remarried when I was 15. There's alcoholic tendency in my family, and a history of incest and many of my family members have been involved in relationships outside of marriage.

The baby I had was not my husband's, she was the product of an extramarital affair. I was a very confused person. I was always looking for someone to love me, to listen to me, and my relationship with my husband, David, had reached a kind of boredom, a stage where we didn't seem to have the facilities within ourselves to reach out to each other. So I went to this other man I met at work, Mitchell. It was one of those situations where he kept pushing me, wanting things to go further and I tried to push him off. He also was married, had two children and was almost 10 years older than I. Finally, I caved in and slept with him on several occasions.

I didn't think I was able to bear children because I have a disease called endometriosis, so you can imagine what a shock it was when I found out I was pregnant and didn't know who the baby belonged to—David or Mitchell. Just before I suspected I was pregnant, David found out about the affair. I moved out, going to my parents' home and there, two weeks later, I took a home pregnancy test.

When I first had the test done, my mom went with me to the store, and I told her I was going to get the test and she said, "Well I really think you're pregnant, but why don't you wait for a few days?" She could tell by the look on my face. They say a pregnant person glows, but I didn't feel like I was glowing!

We went to the store, got the test, went home and it came out positive, but when I walked out of the bathroom, I entered my state of denial. My jaw was on the floor and my mom said, "What's going on? Is it positive?" And I said, "Yes, it is, but maybe it's wrong." The first thing I thought is, "Oh no, I can't be pregnant," so a day or two later I decided to pay for a pregnancy test at the doctor's office. I went to one of those emergency clinics. They did a urine test; again it came out positive and again I was quite stunned. I still was going through a state of denial.

I asked the nurse to send the doctor in because I

wanted to ask him about having a paternity test done. My thought was, "What am I going to do now?" I assumed David and I would raise the child whether or not David was the biological father.

At that point, I didn't consider any option other than keeping the baby. Abortion went through my mind but not for long. I knew I couldn't live with myself if I had an abortion to make my life easier. There were religious considerations as well as several friends who had abortions told me about the physical and emotional consequences. There is no way I would do that to myself, I'd have nightmares for the rest of my life. That may be a selfish reason for not choosing abortion, but in the long run abortion would have so much guilt attached.

I called my husband and told him about the positive test. He said, "I hope to God that baby is mine." His reaction stunned me because always before David had taken everything I dished out. He would jump right back with, "Donna, I love you"...and everything would be all right. I thought that was how this would go. So that was my first connection with reality. I thought, "Oh shit. What am I going to do? He won't be Dad unless he *is* Dad biologically."

In the meantime, I'm puking my guts out every day; for eight weeks straight, I'm over the toilet all morning, usually until afternoon when I would go to work. I was still thinking, "This can't be happening to me." At my second doctor's appointment, it began to be real to me when the doctor said, "We're going to see if we can hear the heartbeat today."

It was unbelievable and I started shedding a lot of tears. At 10 weeks old, the heartbeat could be heard! David was anxious to have a paternity test done in vitro, even though several doctors told us it wasn't possible until the baby was born. He was pushing me to have the in vitro test done at 12 weeks. I was getting pressure at both ends because I was still in contact with Mitchell, who told me, "If this is my baby, I want to raise it."

I thought: "Bull. There's no way you're going to raise this child." He was separated from his wife at that point, so it was easy for him to say, "I'll raise it." But what about his other two kids, I was thinking. David insisted, "If this is my baby, I want it."

Finally, I sat back and thought, then told both of them, "Wait a minute. I'm the one carrying this child; I'm the one who is going to actually deliver this child and have the maternal feelings for it. You guys are not going to dictate to me what I do in my life."

I decided that David and I needed to figure out together whether we were ready, really prepared to raise a child regardless of whose child it was. If we were not, it seemed to me that adoption was the best choice for the baby. My main objective then was to keep my marriage together; I had made a commitment to my husband for life and then had broken it by having an affair. David asked me, "Do you love Mitchell?"

I had to answer that I honestly didn't know if I loved Mitchell or not. I had feelings for him, cared for him—but love? I knew I loved David dearly, and I had hurt him. Together, as "we," a decision had to be made about the baby and it was clear that David and I were in no position to raise a child.

Three months into the pregnancy, David and I decided to place the baby for adoption, with no paternity tests done. David had already been saying there was no way he would raise Mitchell's child; now he was saying, "We don't have the kind of stable marriage that is needed to raise a child." I refused to consider that I might be giving away David's baby.

Once that decision for placement was made, I began looking into the different types of adoption. Whether I should go through an agency, a private adoption through an attorney and in what state... I checked the library for books on adoption, which wasn't very helpful because most were directed at teen mothers. I was 24 years old and my reasons for choosing adoption were not the same as a 17-year-old's. I began to feel guilty. A 17-year-old has every right to place a baby for adoption, her whole life is ahead of her—school...My reasons were more that the pregnancy caused me problems and that giving the baby away would make everything O.K. That didn't seem a good reason; I felt very selfish for wanting the baby out of my life.

Not that I didn't love my child. I knew it wasn't the baby's fault. In some way, I thought adoption would solve my problem. At that point, three or four months along, I still didn't know how attached I would become to the child, the emotions I would have with letting her go.

My first choice was an intra-family adoption, a cousin who had six miscarriages and whom I saw only once or twice a year. That way I could see the child occasionally. But my cousin said no, she didn't advocate open adoption. My next choice was a friend, not one close to me but someone close to my brother. Arrangements were made for my brother to introduce me to this couple, Don and Pat who live about two hours away from David and me. First I talked to Don by phone, learning they had one adopted child and were very much interested in another.

Don and Pat agreed to meet with me and to send a lot of photos of the child to me, which they were also doing with their first birthmother. I let them know I wanted an open adoption, that I wanted to be able to keep in some kind of contact with the child. Don was

O.K. with that—Pat said, not in so many words, but through the tone of her voice, "No way." She did say to me, "I wouldn't want you in my house or anything like that."

Pat's definition of "openness" was sending a lot of pictures. Mine was totally different. I decided to keep looking for couples who would be open to contact after placement. The agencies I contacted in two states were pretty closed, not believing in open adoption, but it turned out that the agency Don and Pat had worked with for their first child would do open adoptions. Because of distance, I spoke with their caseworker mostly by phone while I went to some counseling in my city.

When I was seven-months pregnant, I met with Don and Pat in a restaurant. She was beginning to think along my lines. They took me to visit their home and I felt very good about that since they still didn't know if the baby woud actually be theirs. We agreed finally that I would get to see the baby once a year, that if the baby should die, I would be notified and if they should get divorced, I would be told. Not that I could have done anything about a divorce or death, but I would know. How often and how many pictures they sent me wasn't specified because I trusted them.

It didn't matter to me that Don and Pat already had a little girl. It seemed great that she was adopted too. If she had been a biological child, I would not have placed with them because I think a couple would not be able to help feeling differently about an adopted child and a biological child. That's my own pet peeve. Since Don and Pat could not have biological children, I felt I could give them the child of their dreams.

I was in periodic contact with Don and Pat through the rest of the pregnancy. When I felt the baby move the first time, about 20 weeks, I called them. When I was due for an ultrasound, I asked them if they wanted to know the sex—Pat said, "no"; Don said, "yes." I felt pretty detached still from the baby, but that all changed when I saw the ultrasound. My mom was with me; the nurse said she thought it was a girl. I felt butterflies in my stomach. Before I had thought, "Oh, that's the baby moving." Now I knew it was my daughter.

Giving up a girl, I knew, was going to be harder for me than a boy would have been. I had always pictured myself someday as the mother of a girl, with a husband, and a house—the white picket fence idea! The perfect scenario. It's not realistic, but I pictured a daughter growing up to be mommy's friend. When I went back to work that day I told myself, "Get used to the idea you're giving away your baby girl, your first child. You'll never be able to say that you've not had kids before. You're giving away this child." The more I thought about it, the more I asked, "Can you really do this, Donna?" I definitely started wavering.

Later that day, I called Don and said, "Well, it's a girl." He was excited...actually Don and Pat were the only people ever excited or happy about my pregnancy. That helped make me happy, but I also felt guilty because they were taking the chance of getting to know me, getting excited about a child that I could still decide to keep.. They seemed so pleased to be expecting their second child! I should have been honest and told them I was wavering. I regret that now—not that it hurt our relationship, but they should have known I was, at that point, reconsidering.

I began to think: "If it's David's, I should keep this baby." When I told David my feelings had changed, he was really pissed off. He said, "First you make a commitment to our marriage and you back out on that, you go screw around with somebody else. Now, we've made a commitment to giving away this child and you're backing out on that one too."

When I told him I wanted the paternity test done after all, that if the baby girl was his, I wanted to keep her, David was so angry that he went to see a priest about divorcing me or getting an annulment. Then he went to an attorney, who advised him to do something quickly because, in my state, I could have gotten child and support money whether the child was his biologically or not. I was still living with my parents. In the state where David and I have a home, he only would have had to pay support if the child was his. Fortunately, David decided not to pursue divorce.

He said to me, "I feel like you're going to use the baby as a pawn to get me back, but I'll agree that if she is mine, we'll keep her." David and I knew it would be hard working on our marriage, getting over an affair and being parents, but I moved back into our home after being separated from David for seven months. Immediately we made arrangements for the paternity test. Mitchell had also reunited with his wife and, at first, he refused to have his blood tested.

By law, Mitchell didn't have to cooperate, but eventually he agreed to do it, provided it wouldn't cost him any money. That made me mad. The test ran over $1,500. What they do is draw blood from the men and the woman and from the embryonic fluid. The stuff is grown in cultures, DNA matching is looked for and it's 99 percent accurate. I will never forget the day the results came in—November 26, 1990. It was 4:30 P.M. David had gotten home early from work and we were taking a nap, when the phone rang.

In essence the woman said, "Donna, we're 99 percent certain your husband is not the father of this child." She went on to say, "Don't take that to mean that the other man is definitely the father." I found that sickly amusing, thinking, "Well, if he's not the father, I sure don't know who else could be." I had been praying the baby would be David's, wondered how we were going to get through this, how our marriage could survive.

"David," I said, "it's not your baby." He started crying and I felt rotten, the one person who was supposed to be his best friend, his wife, and I had done this to him. Right away, he called his mother and talked to her. It was hard to take that he couldn't turn to me. I knew then that the baby could not be mine either. Even if I could never have another child, I didn't want to lose my marriage. Maybe that's a selfish reason for finally choosing adoption. If David had divorced me or if David had suddenly died, maybe I would have chosen to raise the baby. I can honestly say I'm glad neither of those events happened. That same evening, David and I went to a movie, trying to get our minds off the baby situation and when we returned home, I learned my grandfather had died. Needless to say, it was really a bad day. All at once, I lost not only my baby but my grandfather. My belief in God helped me from there till delivery, even though in the past I had often turned my back on God. I tried to pray each day, taking one day at a time with his help.

David was my coach through Lamaze and he agreed to be with me in labor, all making me think how wonderful it would have been if she had been his baby. I went into labor on December 23rd. Immediately I called Pat and Don, who were visiting relatives for the holiday, more than six hours away. They knew all about the paternity test the month before and they knew that if the baby had been David's we were going to keep her, but they never wavered in their interest.

That night there was a big snowstorm, so Pat and Don decided to drive to the hospital in the morning. After my water broke, intensive labor began six or seven hours later. By then I was sick of it all. I wanted that baby out of me. I was tired of carrying around 30 extra pounds, tired of having a baby laying in bed between my husband and me, tired of a pregnancy screwing up our whole relationship. I decided not to name the baby and didn't feel then that I had any maternal emotion.

Jessica was born at 12:32 in the afternoon of December 24th. David was right there with me, but we had agreed we would not hold the baby so I stuck to that. Don and Pat arrived about 6 o'clock, came in the room, and I picked the baby up for the first time, handed her to Pat and said, "Here is your baby." They stayed about five hours, holding her, and I was very happy for them. They chose the name Jessica.

Our plan was that I would leave the hospital with Jessica and meet Don and Pat at a hotel. We had no attorney or social worker present, our relationship was very trusting, but I don't know that was a wise way to do it. Because it was Christmas, we just didn't get other people involved at that point. I left the hospital on December 25th, so I could celebrate Christmas with David, returned for Jessica on the 26th. Don and Pat provided clothing and a car seat. My mom went with David and me to the hospital. I agreed not to hold the baby in front of David, so he waited while I dressed Jessica. From the hospital to the hotel, she sat beside me in her car seat.

Going up the elevator, my mom held Jessica. We got to Don and Pat's room and she put Jessica on the bed. My mom got all emotional, crying; then David started crying and I lost it too. It was very painful for everyone. I think I said something like, "Please be good to her." Then I picked Jessica off the bed and gave her to Pat, saying, "Merry Christmas."

"This is the best Christmas present anyone could ever get," Pat replied. I believe it was and even though it felt like my heart was being ripped out, I knew it was the right thing to do. It hurt like hell. Legally, Jessica was still mine. Pat and Don had to trust me, that I wasn't going to back out. I trusted them to take care of her from that moment on.

It was January 10th before I signed the final papers because at the agency there was only one caseworker who would do an open adoption. David also had to sign as the legal father and Mitchell had to sign as the biological father, a pretty weird case. Afterwards it was pretty rough—both for me and my husband. Our relationship had been hit hard by the pregnancy and the affair and we are still working on it. I attend a support group for birthmothers and I'm very interested in being an advocate for open adoption.

The first year I saw Jessica three times. David will not go with me. I don't know how it's going to work once we have kids because I would want them to know Jessica too. Don and Pat seem to be O.K. with that idea. I used to be scared they would suddenly change their minds and not let me see Jessica anymore. As time has passed, the trust between us has grown.

We work on little things that could be problems as time goes on—like once Pat said, "*When* Jessica asks about you...or *if* Jessica asks about you"...I don't want it to be *if* and *when*. I am her birthmother. Right now. And forever. I know she won't understand for a long time what that means, but I want her to know the word. I am not a family friend, so to speak, in the usual sense. I'm not an aunt. If she hears the word "birthmother," it won't be startling to her later on. I think Don and Pat agree with this now.

Another thing that bothers me is when everyone else talks about "letting go." My family members are uncomfortable when I talk about my visits to Jessica and people who have not placed a baby for adoption talk about "getting on with your life." It is not possible to "let go" of something like this. The similarity is with my grandfather's death. I can think of the good times I had with him and also the bad times. Because he is gone doesn't mean he doesn't exist for me. The same is true for Jessica. I gave birth to her and there were good moments and bad moments. Because she is in another family doesn't mean she ceased to exist for me.

I should be able to talk about the good things of adoption and the openness allows for that. I am proud of my daughter by birth. I can walk through baby departments without feeling all upset because I know where Jessica is. She's not 100 percent missing from my life. Looking at my friends' newborns doesn't hurt as much because I know how my birthdaughter is developing. She isn't a "baby" forever in my mind.

The first holidays were very hard—Mother's Day, the first birthday. It would have been nice if Don and Pat had sent me a card or a note on those days. I would advise adoptive couples to do that. Sometimes it hurts to think I am missing out on so much of my child's life; I worry that I may not ever have another child with David, but overall I think I made the right decision. If I had raised my baby, I would have been working 40 hours a week, coming home late and dealing with a child. That seems to be the norm nowdays—day care, babysitters...but I wouldn't have liked that for my child. Overall my relationship with Pat, Don, Jessica and her sister has been very positive. Together we attend a support group for families with an open adoption and recently Pat said to everyone, "We feel Donna is part of our family."

Tears of joy came to my eyes and I felt my prayers had been answered. The adoption was in my best interest, maybe in a selfish way because it enabled me to keep my marriage. It was definitely in Jessica's best interest.

ELIZABETH

"Adoption is better than abortion. My baby only has one life and I wanted to give it to him."

A high school junior at the time of her pregnancy, Elizabeth confided in no one but the baby's father. She was never ambivalent about her decision to carry her child to term or place him for adoption. A slim young woman with dark eyes and long dark hair, Elizabeth hoped her honor roll standing in school would enable her to attend a good college, intending one day to study law.

When her labor began, Elizabeth's parents took her to the hospital, thinking her "stomach pains" were the symptoms of appendicitis. Her son weighed 6 lbs. A hospital social worker notified an adoption agency of Elizabeth's desire to place the infant who went to foster care for 13 days. On the day Elizabeth and Steven, her boyfriend, signed their relinquishments, she asked only that she be allowed to know the first name chosen for her birthson by the adoptive couple and that she be able to give her baby a last kiss.

Elizabeth graduated from high school a year later, was accepted to the college of her choice but was unable to put together enough funds combined with a student loan to attend. She now works full-time, planning to attend a local college in the future.

ɕ

I am the youngest in my family. My brother is oldest, then my sister, who is five years older than I. My dad is an alcoholic, so I put up with a lot of name calling and abuse though my brother got the worse of it. He and dad were constantly at each other. My mom really got the bad end, she had so many threats made on her. She worked in a factory nights; my dad worked days and he was supposed to be taking care of us, but my sister was stuck raising me. It was hell to be around our house.

My sister had to clean and take care of me; she had a hateful attitude then and we were not at all close. My brother never helped her; he just came and went as he wanted. I was sort of stuck in the middle of everything. Once my mom went to file for a divorce, the judge talked her out of it. He made them reconcile. I don't know if that was for the best or the worst!

What could my mom do? She had three kids. She could have lived with her parents, but that would have been an awkward situation. School was about all I had, that's why I was a good student. I didn't really hang around anybody, it was just, more or less, school for me. I hated alcohol and drugs, shied away from anybody like that. I didn't want drunks for friends. My sister had her friends and I had school.

Surprisingly, my dad supported me in my schooling even though he was drinking. He always believed in getting a good education because he didn't get to finish school. Then my dad did a complete turnaround and our lives changed. We made him quit drinking. The whole family left him and after four days he wanted to talk to my mom and they got everything straightened out. They dumped all his beer. He didn't touch any for two weeks; after that he had a few each day. He will admit he drinks a lot, but he won't fully admit that he has really got a problem. At least he doesn't break out in his babbling rages, so he does really good now.

I started dating in eighth grade, about 13 years old. I wouldn't call it heavy dating, just going to the mall or a friend's house. I met Steven in my freshman year. He's two years older than me. We had a class together, ceramics. He really wanted to study it seriously, go to college, but his mom couldn't afford to send him. His childhood wasn't the greatest either, divorced parents, and his brother is into cocaine. Steven won't even acknowledge him.

We were friends for a year and a half, then we started dating and it just went on from there. We have never broken up. We can talk openly and we enjoy each other's company, just little things like going to the beach, playing pool. We get along great. I'm not looking for a commitment, an engagement or anything like that.

I got pregnant a month or two before my 16th birthday. It wasn't planned. Every weekend his mother would leave, ever since Steven was old enough to take care of himself. She would go away on weekends. We were at his house, we used condoms, but they didn't work. There are certain things you don't think you can talk to your parents about—like birth control or telling your parents that you are having sex with somebody. They would probably go through the roof so you try to find someone else to talk to.

The only person I told was Steven. First there was that suspicion I was pregnant, then a denial period and then he accepted it. I told Steven, "I'm going to put the baby up for adoption." Abortion was out of the picture. I never considered it. It was totally my decision. By then I was in my fourth or fifth month.

I was scared. Real scared. It came to either I keep the baby or give him up for adoption. Steven asked my why and I told him: "The baby wouldn't have a future with me, wouldn't have a stable home, wouldn't have both parents." Steven agreed with me. He preferred adoption too because he couldn't be there as a full-time father for the baby. He wanted to avoid one parent raising a baby. Nobody on Steven's side knows about the baby even now.

If I had to do it over again I would tell my parents about the pregnancy and get all the medical care, but as far as adoption goes, I wouldn't change that. It was the best decision all the way around for everybody. As it was, I got an ulcer worrying, trying not to look pregnant. I didn't starve myself, I tried to eat well knowing the baby woud need all he could get. I've always had trouble gaining weight anyhow so that was not a problem. All together I gained about 11 lbs.

Basically I had to worry about walking from class to class. My gym credits were taken care of already so I was O.K. there. I made the honor roll too. I'm really lucky that everything turned out O.K. The grace of God was over me. I think there was a purpose for everything that happened; this didn't happen by itself. I believe a lot in God, that he has taken part in everything with me.

I saw my son for about three minutes after he was born. I think I'll always remember him, laying in the little crib-like thing in the hospital with his little blue hat on. I can see him just like that. At the agency I saw him again when I signed adoption papers. I held him there, too, for a while and so did my mom. He has Steven's blue eyes, but as far as looks go, I don't know who he looks like. Over a year, his family sent a few pictures. The only thing I got upset about was they wouldn't send a full face picture so I can see how he looks. His side view is cute but I'd like to see how he looks from the front, how big his hands are...I don't know their names. I don't know anything about them except what they like to do and that they are taking good care of him.

I tried writing them through the agency and told them I would never do anything to harm them, I'm not that kind of person. If they ever talked to me, they would find that out. I don't know what else they want from me. I'm glad his parents are protective of him; I'd rather he be real spoiled than to ever feel neglected. If he's a healthy, happy little stinker, I think that's great. I don't regret my choice. I believe his family loves him and I can live with not knowing them.

When they write letters, I like it because I can see how they are interacting with him, how he is doing. That's my biggest concern, that he is all right. My first Christmas was very hard, wondering if he was opening gifts, playing with a train or what. But I am, I think, just normally concerned about what is happening to my child. I'm not obsessed with wondering. I've accepted my decision and I deal with myself on the down days. In my opinion, adoptive parents shouldn't be so paranoid about birthparents, thinking someone is out there constantly looking for their child. It's not that I'm stone cold, I know when to let go.

I don't feel guilty for my decision. Right after I signed the papers, I went through a period where I was pissed at everybody, my emotions were so wrecked... I'd be happy one day and so depressed the next day. It wasn't directed at any particular person. I'd think about the baby every day; then after a few weeks, I pulled myself together. Sometimes, I feel selfish because I wanted to go to school instead of taking care of a baby.

Some of my friends had babies and kept them. Their parents have to help out, but as far as their boyfriends go, they are long gone. The girls are stuck on their own and it's too much for them. They're always bitching and in a bad mood. I see people walking around with one-two-three kids and they can't take care of them properly. I feel I did the right thing for my baby.

Someday I think my baby will be curious about who he looks like or where he gets certain traits from. If he looks for me, I'd tell him not to judge people too quickly, that would be the main thing. I hope he will believe in God and grow up able to make his own decisions. I hope he'll understand how I came to make my decision.

MARY KAY

"Once you give someone your baby, you feel close to them, so how can you just break it off and go live your life while they go live theirs?"

The youngest of seven children, Mary Kay's good looks and gregarious personality cover a lot of personal anguish. A brother has been diagnosed as schizophrenic and confined to an institution. Believing family members perceived her as "their sweet little girl," Mary Kay was frantic when she realized she was pregnant. Though contact with an adoption agency was made during her second month, Mary Kay experienced great pressure for an intra-family adoption up to the day she signed relinquishments.

In selecting her birthdaughter's family, Mary Kay wanted a full-time mother with both parents coming from large families. After Adrienne's placement in September 1989, Mary Kay corresponded regularly with the adoptive parents, receiving many photos with each letter. In October of 1991 Mary Kay and her husband of nine months had dinner with Adrienne's parents. A letter written to them by Mary Kay follows her story.

❦

I was 17 when I met him in high school. My best friend introduced us. About three months after we became friends, we started dating—right after my 18th birthday. I remember being so much in love with him; he was so shy and I was too, but he was totally shy for a guy. I liked his blue eyes. My mom liked him a lot too.

After we dated a while, there was a lot of pressure to have sex because it was prom time—May. Everybody was saying to me, "You got to have sex." When senior prom time came up, I said to him, "Randy, I'm not ready to have sex," and he said, "Neither am I."

It wasn't peer pressure, it was that—all my girlfriends had been dating their guys for so long that all of them were already having sex. They all thought prom night would be the perfect time, but I didn't want to do it on prom night, so Randy and I just had a nice time at the prom and the next day we didn't go to the beach with everybody. I went to a family baptism.

Randy and I could talk about everything. That's why I liked him so much, though he wasn't as cute as most of the guys I dated. He was so very nice to me. I remember everybody thought we were going to get married; we really were the cutest couple. It was sometime in July that we became sexually active. I didn't think I could become pregnant because my two sisters had a lot of female problems. I spent the entire summer with Randy after graduation. He lived on a lake and we spent every day together, swimming, water skiing, canoeing. We had so much fun together! We were friends and boyfriend-girlfriend. That summer was one of the hottest summers, 100 degrees everyday.

In September I started my freshman year of college. Because Randy was working full time we didn't see much of each other—not like we did in high school and I dated some other guys briefly. In November I had to have surgery on my leg. When I was a small child, I was burned in an accident and this was the beginning of a series of plastic surgery. Randy came to see me in the hospital. It took him two hours of driving to get there. I remember my period started the day of the surgery, but the next month, December, there was no period.

I was upset and worried. On New Year's Eve, I drank screwdrivers and felt really queasy. That never happened before. I don't usually get drunk and throw up, but the drinks made me so sick that I got the chills real bad, so I quit drinking. I remember I spent the night with Randy. About two weeks later I was supposed to get my period. When I didn't get it, I took a pregnancy test, found out that I was pregnant. I was hysterical.

I called Randy up and said, "I'm pregnant." We were supposed to go out together that night, but he said something so stupid that I wanted to kill him. I drove to his house to get some clothes I had left there. That whole month, I was hysterical. I was beating my stomach, crying... I didn't know what my mother was going to do after she found out I was pregnant.

Randy and I stayed together for only a month and a half after that. I was three-and-a-half months pregnant and we celebrated our 19th birthdays. Then he went on a skiing trip, came back and said, "I don't want to talk to you anymore, I don't want to date you anymore." We didn't talk for a month and then he called me, told me he loved me and all this other stuff, and he wanted to meet me for lunch the next day. I got all excited, but he never called again. So after that I thought, "Screw you," deciding I was never going to talk to him again.

Later I left a letter on his pillow saying I was going to give the baby up for adoption and I didn't want to see him anymore and I think his mom found the letter. That's one reason I wrote it because I wanted her to read it. I wanted her to know, but I didn't want to tell her.

I told one of my guy friends, John, who was in the Navy. I called him and told him I was pregnant by Randy and that adoption was best for the baby. John called his mother and asked her to help me. She made an appointment for me at an adoption agency and went with me. That day I left a note for my mom. It said, "I'm pregnant and I'm at such and such an agency."

My mom freaked out. She wanted me to give the baby to one of my two sisters. And she was hurt I didn't tell her first, but neither one of us could tell my dad. He figured it out by himself because all of a sudden I was going to bed at 9 o'clock and I never went out anymore. I lost weight because I was so nervous. I was four months pregnant, my usual weight is 122, but I was down to 117 and my friends were telling me I was too skinny.

I decided to go live with one of my sisters for the last part of the pregnancy, after school was finished, then come back home in time for the next semester. I knew it would work out that way. Just before I left home, my dad and I were watching TV together, when he turned to me and said, "What do you want, a boy or a girl?"

I said, "Who told you I was pregnant?" My dad just said, "I don't know what to think about Randy." It was difficult, here it was Randy's baby and he never got to feel her move around...maybe guys that age don't think about stuff like that, maybe they don't care. Randy could have had a wife and a baby, but he didn't give it a chance. Later he told me, "We wouldn't have made it together."

It takes two people to raise a baby, emotionally and financially. I never really thought about keeping my baby. I wanted to go to college, I didn't want to raise a baby. What kills me is when I see people who don't care about their kids, who think if you get pregnant, you have to have the baby and go on welfare. I know a lot of nice people who are on welfare, but I don't think teenagers know how hard it is to raise a baby. It's cute to have a baby, but a baby is a lot of work.

The last part of my pregnancy, when I was with my sister and her family, was happy. I felt on top of the world, spent a lot of time lying in the sun in a bikini. I wanted my stomach to get tan even though my bikini looked like it was going to explode on me! I made a blanket for the baby and started to crossstitch it. My friends who came to visit would ask, "Why are you making all this? Are you going to keep the baby?" I'd say, "No, I want her to have this." They'd respond, "I know you are making all this so you can keep the baby, and I kept on saying, "I'm not keeping the baby. I'm just making it so it can go with her."

The pressure not to choose adoption was terrible. Both of my sisters really wanted the baby, but I couldn't choose between them. I talked with a priest and a woman who placed a baby for adoption and that helped. I didn't want to be "Aunt Mary Kay" to my own baby at every family gathering.

The day Adrienne was born, I remember, I had an upset stomach and my back was killing me. I took a shower, noticing I had pains 13 minutes apart but when I came out of the shower, they were six minutes apart, then two minutes, then back to six. I thought, "This can't be it. The pains are supposed to be five minutes apart for about two hours." That's what they said at Lamaze class! But I woke up my sister with, "I don't know if I'm in labor or not!"

The hospital was an hour away. She drove 90 mph to get there; the pains were maybe 20 seconds apart and it seemed like we parked two miles away from the door. I carried my luggage in, stopping every other minute, putting it down because I was having contractions right on top of each other and when I got to the nurses' station on the maternity floor, the baby kicked real hard. My water broke, I didn't want to tell anyone, thinking I had peed my pants.

I didn't have any drugs during labor, it was a wonderful experience. After my water broke, the labor intensified 50 million times! I remember the doctor telling me to push, but I was faking...I could see his head and glasses between my legs and I wanted to kick him! I was so tired. The doctor said, "Her head and shoulders are out. Come down here and pull her out." I said, "No, you pull..." He grabbed my hands and made me pull her out and I thought she was going to be a five pound baby but she was eight pounds! I couldn't even lift her up to my chest. She knew who I was because she stopped crying as soon as she saw me. For half an hour I held her while my sister was snapping pictures like crazy.

I kept on thinking to myself, "I'm your aunt." I was always Aunt Mary Kay to my nieces and nephews, so I kept myself distant by saying, "Aunt Mary Kay loves you so much." At the same time I was thinking, "Oh my God, this is my baby." It helped to think that I was just her aunt, but it also delayed my reaction, kept pushing the feelings away.

The whole time I was in the hospital, I did not cry, but I could not sleep. I looked like somebody had beat me up because I had black circles under my eyes and I was all white. What was really hard was when my mom came to the hospital with the car seat like we should keep the baby and my sister was the same way. She said, "Mary Kay, you can't give this baby up. You're not going to be able to handle it. You don't know what it's like to have a child."

I kept myself distant from the baby even though I washed her up in the nursery and had her in my room. One day I fell asleep with her in my arms, in two hours I woke up and she was still sleeping. I didn't know if I was supposed to wake her up. I didn't know anything about babies. I thought, "What's wrong with her. She sleeps all the time."

She really was a good baby and leaving her at the hospital was very difficult. That morning I got up real early, got her from the nursery. It was barely 6:00 A.M. and we watched the sun rise together. For some reason I wanted her to remember that day. That was the only time I saw her really awake. When I got dressed to leave, I sat on the bed, trying to suck my stomach in so my outfit would fit, the nurse said, "I have to walk with you out of the hospital."

I asked, "What are you going to do with the baby?" She was going to foster care because I had signed temporary papers, but I meant that exact moment. The nurse said she'd put her back in the nursery. I said, "No, leave her in the room. I don't want her to follow me out." There on the maternity floor, it felt like everybody was walking by, like they were looking for a baby. It was terrible, leaving her in the hospital.

My sister picked me up in the car, all her kids with her and my niece asks, "Where's the baby?" I didn't say anything. The next two days at my sister's, hell I didn't talk to anybody. It was very quiet. My sister treated me kind of shitty because they all disapproved of my decision. I wanted to call my best girlfriend and tell her I had a little girl, but my sister snapped, "Call her when you get home."

I remember being so numb. I tried to make an educated decision to give the baby up, but other people don't care; it makes me really mad. I chose a family for the baby, reading letters from couples. I was scared I wouldn't like any of them, but one just stood out. Before I'd never noticed how difficult it was to be an adult. I wished I were a little kid again, to start everything all over. I would know so much.

The week before I signed the final papers, I tried to get Randy to come with me, but all his friends were telling him not to sign. He didn't understand what it all meant, if he'd have to pay or what. You'd think he would have spent some time to learn. I went to see him and I could see he was confused and hurt. We talked for over an hour. He stood like he was going to give me a hug and I kind of pushed him away. Then he asked me if I would go out sometime!

How he could have had that nerve! "You don't

even know how much shit I've gone through the last nine months," I told him. "You just walked away from all of it." It really made me mad; he hadn't changed at all in those nine months. I wanted to do something to him. During the pregnancy I still had the keys to his Mustang, boy did he love that car. That was his baby. He was always working on it and I wanted to do something to hurt him.

I know Randy does feel bad about the pregnancy and the adoption...but I know it doesn't affect him the same way it affects me because he was never around. I think he feels guilty, that's all he feels. He doesn't feel the loss of the child, he just feels guilty that he wasn't there. I asked him, "What do you want me to do because I have made a decision. You run away from everything."

My baby was 19 days old when I went to the agency to sign the final papers. I was in a daze when I signed those papers. I just wanted to get it over with. I made this decision and I didn't want to change my mind and I thought if I gave myself more time, I'd change my mind. During the pregnancy, I felt close to God for some reason. I'd never felt close to him before, but that day, I didn't feel the same. I couldn't pray and I didn't want to go into church anymore. I tried to think positive, but I was scared. One book I read said a high percentage of people in psychiatric hospitals were adopted children, they didn't know who they were.

The couple I chose agreed to send me pictures and letters. They had been married nine years so I felt they had really built their relationship and that both of them really wanted a baby. I could tell they loved each other, understood each other by what they wrote. They send me beautiful pictures. I really wanted to see what Adrienne looked like, not because I wanted to go steal her; I just had that curiosity. When the pictures would come in the mail, I could barely get the envelope open fast enough. At first, I almost sat by the mail box waiting...wondering, "Why don't they send more?"

I knew they were busy. They sent photos of themselves too and she looks, just looks like a mother. Very calm, very earthy. Together they are a cute couple and I could tell Adrienne would be a daddy's girl too because he spends so much time with her. A lot of couples might have been perfect, but they were the best.

I showed Adrienne's picture to Randy's mother, gave her one, and she cried and cried, "She's so beautiful." She said Randy wanted one too and had asked her if he did the right thing. She said to him, "What did you do?" His mom told me that she wished Randy had been more supportive during the pregnancy so I would have kept the baby. The fact is Adrienne looks exactly like Randy and that helped me a lot. To me she looked like a little Randy, a cute little Randy, especially when she had no hair!

Afterwards, I just dealt with it, smoking and drinking. I didn't go out to the bars to meet guys. I went to the bars to see how many guys would look at me. I wore short skirts and halter tops, trying to get every single guy in the bar to look at me. I got off on it and when they would come up to dance I'd say, "I don't want to dance with you. You can look at me but do not touch me."

Everyday I went for two-mile walks; people said to me, "You are so skinny." And I wanted to say, "Well, I just had a baby girl." What can you say to people? I got mad easier because I saw people who had kids and didn't appreciate them. It felt like I cried all the time and I went out every night; my grades at school were terrible. It was like I was trying to run away from my decision.

The night I met the man who is my husband, I was drunk. I was so drunk I don't know what he saw in me. I remember going up to the bar to get a Long Island Iced Tea, two guys were sitting there, telling jokes. I laughed and said "Hi" and Dennis said "Hi" back. I looked at him, thought, "He's kind of cute," so I gave him my number. He gave me his. I told him, "I don't call guys." But I did end up calling him.

Dennis is a very sweet guy and I'm so glad I met him. He helped me. I stopped going out and drinking every night, studied instead and I got straight A's that semester. The first pictures of Adrienne that I showed to Dennis, he got choked up and cried even though she's not his child!

After a while I began to think over every step. I picked out the family for Adrienne. Nobody made that decision for me. I got to take care of Adrienne in the hospital. I bought her things which I could give her through the agency. I could have met her family, but I chose not to because I wanted them to feel they could live their lives and not have to worry about running into me somewhere. Every time I felt like I had made a mistake with the adoption, I thought about the family Adrienne is in and then I didn't feel like I made a mistake.

Dennis and I were married one and a half years after the adoption. I was still going to school full time. Sometimes I wanted to forget about college and have a family, but, no, I want to graduate first. It's hard when people ask if we have kids because I hate saying, "I don't have any children." It's as though I'm ashamed of Adrienne. She's mine and she's not mine. I want to be pregnant again but I want it to be right this time, to be done with school, have a nice house and not have to be sad about being pregnant.

I sent Adrienne's family pictures of Dennis and me and they continued to write and send photos. When we decided to meet, I was so nervous! Dennis and I had dinner with Adrienne's parents; it was wonderful, so nice to have a relationship with them. I thought I might just be opening old wounds and everyone in my family advised me not to do it. I think if everyone is totally truthful, it can be positive. Maybe someday I will meet Adrienne, but I'm not ready yet.

What gets me through it is the same thought that got me through the pregnancy: I know I have made a neat couple happy.

To Adrienne's Parents

You can't believe how happy it made me feel to meet the two of you. All the people I talked to, about meeting with you guys, pretty much discouraged it, but I sure don't have any regrets. Even though I knew you both were great parents, I'm just happy I didn't let a chance of a life time pass me by. Meeting you two just reassured me one more time that I made the right decision. Thanks for being so open. It sure meant a lot.

Love,
Mary Kay & Dennis

Within a year from the time Mary Kay wrote this letter, she and Dennis prepared for the birth of their first child.

Their son was stillborn.

KIM

"Because there was a baby, maybe something good came out of something really awful."

A senior in college, Kim plans to attend graduate school and study psychology. Eventually she wants to be a counselor specializing in trauma. It is obvious that her experience of being the victim of a date rape has greatly influenced her academic choice.

The youngest of three children, Kim describes herself as "quiet, shy and a good student." Her looks, however, are striking. Blonde with blue eyes and a poised manner, Kim recently earned extra spending money through commercial modeling. She has had minimal contact through an agency with her birthson's parents, two letters and three photos. They have chosen not to respond to her request for more information.

❧

I didn't have many close friends my senior year in high school because I had been sick on and off and missed a lot of school. For a week I'd be in school, then I'd be gone. First I was tested for mono and then the doctor said it was chronic fatigue syndrome because it lasted so long. My blood was tested and the antibodies for chronic fatigue were present. I was planning to go to college when I graduated and I had a boyfriend, Chad, who was already away at school. We weren't exclusive. Chad had gone to my high school and we'd been friends for over two years.

Chad and I were waiting till I was ready. He knew I would never sleep with just anybody. I was a virgin; we figured that someday Chad would be the one. What happened was that I was raped on a date. He was a college guy about two years older who seemed fine at first. We went out a couple of times; on the fourth or fifth date I went to his apartment. By then I thought he was a friend. He knew I had a boyfriend and was not looking for a boy-girlfriend situation. I was so naive, should have caught on. I don't know why I was so stupid.

He pushed me, held me down, pressing on my neck. I was crying, telling him to stop, but he was stronger. Afterward I had no intention of ever telling anyone. I just went home. There were bruises on my wrists, it hurt to go to the bathroom and there was a little blood. It never occurred to me that I could be pregnant. I thought something was damaged because it hurt to pee and my next period was spotty so I saw a doctor. He said the spotty period was normal, especially since I'd been ill.

There was some nausea but I never once threw up; again I thought it was the chronic fatigue and I just crawled into bed. My parents didn't think that was odd because it was already going on, sick one week, sleeping a lot, up the second week. I was depressed, crying to myself. About the third month my period stopped altogether, that's when I realized I could be pregnant. Abortion was my first thought. I looked in a medical encyclopedia to see what it would look like at three months. When I saw the pictures, I couldn't do an abortion because it wasn't just a fetus-like thing. Besides I would have had to tell someone. There was no way I could talk about it yet. I didn't want anyone to know anything, just keep it under wraps to myself, live through one day by day.

Each night I would think, "Well, you got through today." I deliberately kept my stomach in, but I ate normally, gained about 25 lbs., mostly at the very end. Chad couldn't understand what was happening with me and with our relationship. I was so emotional all the time, refused to talk to him. I know he was hurt, even though I only saw him a few times during the pregnancy. Since he was away at school both our parents thought it was natural that we drifted apart. My focus was, "Nobody is going to know."

Neighbors suspected I was pregnant, said something to my parents who were pretty indignant at their comments. At the time I was glad it was a big secret, would dream all the time that people would find out. Then I had no intention of keeping the baby, felt no attachment to it, even when I felt it kicking. I thought, "Oh, that's the baby kicking." I never thought of it as mine, didn't want to know what sex it was or ever see it. At the same time, I felt it wasn't the baby's fault, what happened to me. The baby was innocent but was someone else's. Very early I thought adoption was right for the baby.

By my fourth or fifth month, I no longer went to school at all and was an emotional basket case. My parents thought my weight gain was because I slept so much but ate normal amounts of food. About eight months along, my mom suspected and asked me, "Are you pregnant?" I didn't say anything, knowing she would cry. This was her first grandchild. She made an appointment with a counselor and with a female doctor because I didn't want a male to touch me. I didn't want to deal with anyone, was pretending everything was O.K. I refused to tell anyone the name of the guy who raped me because I was very afraid my father and brother would literally kill him. All I wanted was to get the baby out of me so I could go back to school and graduate.

I wasn't attached to the baby in any way until he was born, never expected all that emotion. I wanted to be detached, but my little boy was so beautiful, so miraculous, I couldn't believe that minutes before he had been inside of me. He recognized my voice, looked at me, his eyes full of wonder and innocence. At that moment, I loved him more than anything in the world and didn't know how I could lose him. But I had made my decision and knew deep down that adoption was the right one for both of us.

After delivery, I spent a half hour with him. That may not have been the right decision because that half hour still haunts me, his being my child, completely different from anyone else in the world and completely beautiful. There I was, his mom, and he needed to bond with someone and it should have been me, but I couldn't imagine feeding and caring for a baby if he weren't going home with me. Through adoption I could give him to two parents who were prepared to have a child and who wanted one so badly.

My older sister and her husband offered to raise the baby, but I couldn't have someone raise my child right in front of me. My parents offered to help me parent the baby—after he was born, we thought of every possibility, but how would I have explained to everyone how I got this child? How would I have explained to a child why he didn't have a daddy? I wanted to go to school too; if I didn't, where would I get the money to raise a child? He would definitely be better off with two parents.

The separation was so hard. This was another life, a child who belonged in my own family, an extension of myself, but he couldn't be mine. All I could think about was how I ached to be with him, it was as though a portion of me was missing. I felt empty. It is an agonizing process to decide to give your child up for adoption, to choose whether or not you'll be part of a child's future. Because my baby wasn't the result of an act of love may have made the decision a little easier for me than for other women. In that sense, I feel more fortunate than women who must deal with a boyfriend, a baby's father...when they choose adoption. At least it was completely my own decision.

I had to do a lot of soul searching before I signed the papers to release my baby for adoption. I wanted to hold him in my arms forever, I never expected to love him as much as I did—and still do. I worried that he could have characteristics from his father, psychological ones, that would make something wrong with him too. I worried that if I kept him, he would grow up looking just like his father. How could I deal with that?

Some people think that there is no good reason to give up your child, that the child must someday deal with feelings of being rejected by his/her own mother. My baby will have to deal with that, plus I want him to know there were extenuating circumstances to his birth. On one hand, I want to say to him, "I didn't just decide: sorry, I can't raise you; I was raped, the ultimate violation. I had no control over what happened to me."

On the other hand, it would be awful to know your father was a rapist. How does anyone deal with that? During the pregnancy I would think, "Why am I doing this?" When the emotional pain was unbearable, I thought sometimes that an abortion would take care of everything. Now I feel like a walking pro-life poster. Though I think abortion should be legal because I can't put myself in anyone else's shoes, I can say, would love to say to people, "Look at me, I'm the exception everyone talks about. I was raped. I was pregnant. I didn't kill anyone and I'm relatively okay now."

I signed the adoption papers when my baby was seven weeks old. I read the letter from the couple I chose so many times that I knew it by heart. My mother cried the whole time—she still cries. My father didn't really know what to say to me—he still doesn't, is afraid he'll upset me, I think. My brother seems repulsed by it all, refused to see the baby in the hospital or talk about any of it. I could talk to my mom or my sister about the baby and after the birth, everyone in my family, everyone I was close to, knew about it.

Eventually I told Chad though I had avoided him for so long, acted like I wanted nothing to do with him that we weren't close as we had been. He was like a part of my family though, more like a brother than a boyfriend. I was still very emotional a couple of months after the baby's birth and I couldn't deal with any sort of physical attention. First I told Chad about the rape, not the pregnancy, and he told his father who remarked, "Thank God, she didn't get pregnant."

It was hard on Chad because he knew I hadn't been close with any other guy, that I wouldn't sleep with anybody. He was angry and hurt too because we were always waiting for the right time, till I was ready to have sex. He always thought he would be the one... essentially the rape destroyed or took away my relationship with Chad too.

For at least a year I thought about the baby every single day, wondering how long that was going to last. The second year it got better, I wasn't constantly wondering what he was doing or crying all the time. Pictures and letters from his adoptive parents helped a lot. In one letter they said they loved me because of what I had done and gone through. I never thought they would think of me that way. I thought they would feel like most people seem to feel about rape, that I deserved what happened or that I had led the guy on.

During the first summer I began having nightmares. I didn't tell anyone but then my parents heard me cry out. It was like all the emotion and hurt was coming up, I couldn't hold it down any longer. I was going to a rape counselor, but she didn't seem to help much, she kept wanting me to talk about the rape, keep a journal of my thoughts, but how many times can you write, "I hate you." I didn't know what to do with my anger. I knew that the guy who raped me was in R.O.T.C. and I kept hoping he'd get sent to Saudi Arabia and get killed.

One thing my rape counselor said off-hand did help me. That was, "A rape affects your life, changes it, but it doesn't have to ruin it." I did a lot of reading on rape, trying to comprehend why anyone would do such an act. I know it's power, not sex. Some people compare it to a mugging, but it's more than that. It seems like only someone who has been through a rape can understand what it was like and ignorance doesn't even begin to explain how some people view rape, especially date rape. Even my friends comment, "You shouldn't have led him on." Or the comment, "I know that so and so wouldn't do such a thing."

In essence they're calling the victim a liar. It sounds like psycho-babble but "a victim" was the role I was into, very paranoid, scared, carrying it all around with me. Sometimes I was afraid to be by myself, afraid of a knock on the door. Then I did the opposite, took risks, went for long bicycle rides at night. That was pretty stupid and it scared my mom to death, but it was like I had to find a way to get control of my life again. I even hoped I'd get attacked again so I could win this time. More stupid. I thought about taking martial art lessons, but just watching a struggle between two people on TV was more than I could handle.

One time I was followed by a man when I was out walking. I ducked into an apartment building, thinking, "You are so stupid. What do you think you are going to do?" When I read an article about a rape occurring on the campus, I'd wonder if it was him again, that it was my fault for not reporting him, that it was my lack of courage that caused someone else to be hurt.

When I went away to school, I took a political science class that included a research group on rape and I became very active in that group. We did a survey on our campus to get an idea of the number of rapes; how many were reported; what was done about it by the police or campus security; whether drinking was involved or a party and so forth. Now I know I was pretty naive that year before when I thought the guy I dated was a friend. Now I know some older college guys try to get to the freshmen girls in "the honeymoon period" when girls want so much to be liked, have no experience with college life, maybe no experience with alcohol or partying. They don't have the judgment they'll have later.

I feel a lot smarter now. Everyone in my research group had a story to tell. For example, we learned most date rapes are dismissed as a dispute between two people. It's not treated like a crime, the attitude is: "Forget about it." If it's a stranger, it's not much better because the police can't find the guy. If a rape occurs in a dorm or on campus, it doesn't even show up in general crime statistics.

Thanks to our professor, who is pretty radical and wants action, our group sponsored a rape awareness seminar. Administration wasn't too thrilled, but a lot of people came, men and women...I passed out flyers and when people looked at me weird, I was reminded how unpopular a topic rape is. While I was uncomfortable, I slowly began to feel I was doing something very important, something to help others and to help myself. I began to get back what I had lost. While I still had nightmares, they weren't about the specific act but about a situation of powerlessness, like someone climbing into my window or stalking me. I go through cycles, cry and try to get it out so I can work again.

Through the group, I met a girl who was raped by her boyfriend. She and my professor are the only two persons I told my entire story to, the rape, the baby and the adoption. It's still very close to me. My friend and I would go home after our meetings with the research group and we would cry together. My friend does a lot of public speaking, but I am not ready for that yet. I am thinking about it.

I also do volunteer work with children the same age my baby would be. Now I wish I had chosen to meet his adoptive parents, in fact, now I would like to see him. I hope he never feels that what happened to me was in any way his fault. If he wants to find me someday, that's fine, but I would not want to impose on his life or be a disturbance in any way. If he's comfortable without ever knowing me, I still won't regret what I did. The adoption was like a death to me, but it was the right decision for him.

On the second anniversary of the rape, I was walking home from the library and suddenly realized that I was wearing the exact same outfit—shirt, shoes, necklace...I don't know how that happened! My first thought was, "How could you have dressed yourself like this on this day?" My second thought was, "Well, my whole body has been shattered, my soul has been ruined, but at least I have managed to fix the necklace that was broken that night."

It's gotten easier, but it's not over. I wonder if it ever will be. I don't date. Once I thought I'd found someone who'd understand, he was supportive whenever I talked about the baby, but how does what happened to me relate to him? How can he feel what I feel?

Recently my sister became pregnant. She asked a lot of questions about my pregnancy but I can't relate. I don't remember when I first felt life because there was no joy then. There was no one to share the exciting things with—like the baby's heart beat. I look at the photos taken of me then and you can't even tell I was pregnant. All the time, I wore a jean jacket. When my sister complains that her pregnancy makes her face break out, I think, "At least you can keep your baby. You planned your baby and you and your husband are really happy about the pregnancy." I was alone.

She wants to share with me, but I can hardly bear to hear it. The rape was one crisis. I have a scar from it that hurts, but the rape wasn't the real crisis in the sense that it was not the most painful crisis. For some reason, it happened and because of it there's a life that's a part of me. But it's a part of me that's missing. I feel like half of me is missing. That's what is so painful, that there is someone out there who is mine, who is part of me. I am more angry about having to give up my child than I am about the attack.

I try to comfort myself, that I gave his parents a great gift. How happy he must make them, but it still hurts. I want someone to tell me that 20 years from now, my baby will be better off because of my decision. Of course, no one can.

CLAIRE

"Looking back, I can see I was a sick person, a psycho and sometimes a little bitch. It's been hard, but I've grown up a lot and learned a lot about myself and relationships. My only regret is that my adoption is not an open one."

Shortly after delivery, Claire's baby daughter, Gabrielle, developed breathing difficulty that kept her in intensive care for several weeks. Upon her release, Claire had every intention of parenting Gabrielle as well as her first daughter Miranda, who was two years old. Her relationship with Gabrielle's birthfather was abusive and volatile to the point that Claire made plans to commit suicide.

Fearing that she might harm her own daughter, Claire made a desperate phone call to her mother who sought assistance from a counselor already involved with the family. Claire was admitted to a psychiatric unit. She agreed to give guardianship of Miranda to her parents and placed Gabrielle in foster care, deciding several weeks later that adoption would be appropriate for Gabrielle.

After reviewing profiles of adoptive couples, Claire selected a family who agreed to maintain contact through letters and photos for two years. She knows Gabrielle's health remains fragile and hopes her family will share information beyond the original period. Almost three years after placing Gabrielle, Claire at 24 has now completed a two-year vocational training program, attends ACOA (Adult Children Of Alcoholics) meetings regularly, is employed full-time and strives to be a good mom to Miranda.

❦

I read a book that saved my life. It was a school assignment my first year in technical training when I had to take a class in human relations. It was about men who treated women like shit, how they put up with it and what steps could be taken to get out of following abusive patterns. Every page in that book was my life and when I went into labor with Gabrielle, I took it with me to the hospital, knowing something would have to change in my life or I would not survive.

My parents are typical, working middle class people. As an only child, I never wanted for anything. The only thing wrong was my dad was an alcoholic. For years I thought it was natural for a man to come home from work late and puke his guts out in the toilet. Hearing my mom cry, listening to them speak their minds, I think I got it in my head that I didn't deserve anything better and that those feelings had a lot to do with how I eventually picked my boyfriends.

Until eighth grade I was a good student, had lots of friends who I let influence me in ways not always good. One girlfriend was five years older, lived next door and she got me started on cigarettes, which later led to pot. Though my parents wouldn't let me date, I was boy crazy and met them at the mall as well as school functions. Honor roll, volleyball—all those good activities—went out the door as I began to skip school. Though I experimented with alcohol, I didn't much like it.

My freshman year, I really started getting into trouble. I liked a 16-year-old boy who lived in our neighborhood. He was a high school dropout, with divorced parents, and he lived with his dad, who was a cocaine head. He smoked pot in front of his dad, which was pretty neat, I thought. Before long, I was smoking too and having sex with him. He came onto me. Other girls I knew were doing it, so why not? At 14 years, I thought that was the way it was supposed to be.

Fourteen is much too early to be sexually active, it just screwed me up further. When my mom found out what I was doing, she wasn't too happy about it. Withdrawal was the only form of birth control we were using and it's still hard for me to believe I was lucky enough not to get pregnant.

About the time my parents learned of the relationship, he moved away (which made them happy), though we wrote to each other for a couple of years. Half-assing my way through high school, I was more into parties and boys than studies. If I liked a class, I could get an A, otherwise C's and D's with no thought to my future. I just got by, living one day at a time, in the moment.

In my sophomore year I got a job as a cashier in a restaurant, became friends with the cook, Joe, who was five years older than I. After six months he told me he had feelings for me, wanted to take me out, meet my parents, which he did. They didn't like the age difference, but Joe was hardworking, not long-haired or smoking like my other boyfriends so they liked him. I thought I loved him, started having sex pretty early. It was in my head: if you date a guy you have sex.

This time my mom took me to get on the pill, but after I began having headaches, I quit taking them. In the back of my head, I knew I could get pregnant but I didn't care. Thinking of the consequences wasn't part of my routine then. Before long Joe and I were fighting a lot. Like a typical Italian male, he was too controlling, telling me what to do and how to dress. I got sick of it. In front of his folks, he wanted me to be a sweet little girl—not that I was a hellion—but lace and pearls wasn't me either.

We'd talk about the future, how someday we'd have beautiful kids together. It sounded good even while we were playing head games with each other. When my periods were spotting, I thought it was stress and went into denial for months. Then I was obviously getting fatter, during my senior year. When I told Joe I was about five months pregnant, he flipped out. That wasn't in his plans.

Together we went to see a counselor. I was crying and very upset. Joe didn't want anything more to do with counseling, wanted me to have an abortion. I wasn't going to do that, I thought adoption was a better option, stuck to that thought. Joe handed me $40 and said, "Do what you want and have a nice life." He left me to deal with myself, an 18-year-old girl with low self-esteem who thought she was shit.

People would say to me, "You're a smart girl," or "You're pretty," but I knew I wasn't 'cause my boyfriend had dumped me. To this day, it's hard for me to build myself up, that negative thinking still holds. I continued in counseling and when my daughter, Miranda was born, my parents fell in love with her.

Up 'til they saw Miranda, they told me, "Do what you want"; then it was, "We'll help you if you bring her home." I signed papers to put Miranda in foster care because I didn't know if my parents were serious. The first night without her in my arms was awful. I couldn't eat or sleep and wanted to kill myself. My dad finally said, "We really want you to keep her."

If I had to live in some dump or on welfare, I would have given her up. I'll always be grateful to my parents for helping me. I called my caseworker, told her, "I can't do this. I want to pick her up in the morning." Within six weeks, I was back at work. Joe never asked about his daughter nor did his parents, who let it be known that they thought I was a whore, having a baby before marrying. He still lives with his mama; he does pay child support because I took him to court to get it.

Miranda knows who her father is. At age four she is beginning to ask questions. We never put Joe down, try to say something like, "Your daddy loves you, but he has a hard time showing it." Recently, I heard his parents have been asking about her, but they don't have the balls to come right out and ask: "Can we see her?" I wouldn't deny them or Joe that opportunity, but they'll have to make the first move because I wouldn't want Miranda to feel rejected ever by them.

Before Miranda was a year old, I was into another relationship. At first I ignored Jose, who was also a cook and older than me by five years! Even his actions and dark hair reminded me of Joe—except Jose was from Mexico. Who needed a repeat? An older waitress intervened, telling me, "He's a nice guy. What's it gonna hurt to go out with him once? If you don't like him..."

Well...I *was* attracted to him so all the red flags popping up were ignored. On our first date, I brought Miranda along. Of course, he was nice. We went out for ice cream. Right away I knew he was the controlling type too and my parents hated him from the first look. Only I was lonely, a single mom, starved for attention and he gave it to me. When I realized he was also dating other women, lying to me, I rationalized, "No big deal. He still cares about me."

As we got closer, the relationship became sicker. Tired of fighting with my parents about Jose, I moved in with him. When I didn't leave a note, they thought Jose took Miranda and me against our will. My dad found out where we were, came over drunk with a gun, trying to protect me. It was nuts! When Jose went at him, my dad shot him in the arm!

Since Jose's papers weren't quite in order, he didn't press charges. Then my parents ran to welfare, trying to get Miranda from me. When the worker came to investigate, our apartment was always clean, Miranda was well dressed, Jose was making good money and I was going to school part-time for medical lab tech. On the outside, things looked good, but Jose was verbally abusive, would tell me one minute, "You're beautiful," the next, "You're too fat," or, "You look retarded wearing that outfit."

I—too—was a conniving little bitch, running back to my parents when life became unpleasant with him. Back and forth, those games went on. A couple of times, Jose got in my face, threatening me physically, but he was skinny, not very tall. "I'll kick your ass if you touch me" was what I told him, but meanwhile, I had no sense of a real life. My schooling was important to me and so was Miranda, who Jose never bothered.

When I realized I was pregnant again, I thought I could make the relationship work somehow, but Jose wasn't happy about it at all. That hurt because I had counted on him caring for us enough to try living together, especially after my first pregnancy alone had been so awful. Jose stayed out late, cheated on me, complaining, "I work 12 hours a day, six days a week while you and your kid just live here, you fucking fat bitch."

I looked for a job, found one in a store and made arrangements for Miranda to go to day care. Inside I was dying, was so psycho-sick that when it was time for my first day of work and Jose pleaded, "Don't go, I'll take care of you," I believed him again. I dropped the job, focused on school and his act changed to, "If you're not going to work, bitch, you can't use the car!"

Every morning I took the bus crosstown to my classes, which were my lifeline, leaving Miranda with my parents. They had gotten legal visitation rights so they also had her on weekends. Eventually, I hated Jose as much as they did, but what other choice did I have? We went months without having sex while he ran around, being real shitty with me. Around then is when I found the book about bad relationships and it became my savior.

Through this whole time, I planned to keep

Gabrielle and when my water broke, I called Jose who said it was my responsibility. My grandmother took me to the hospital, I called Jose again. "Are you coming here?" When he arrived, all he did was check out the nurses so I told him, "Just leave—you're not helping."

My labor was long and hard. Sometime during the night, I called Jose a second time. "What do you want? I'm trying to sleep," he mumbled.

That made me so mad, I replied with something like, "You fucking asshole. This is *your* baby and it's really starting to hurt bad."

"See what you get, bitch, for spreading your legs!"

This comment tore through my heart like a knife. Right there I knew I was leaving him for good. I understood he was a mean person in a way I had not before, even though I'd always known he was married with a wife and child in Mexico, plus another child with someone else in the U.S. Why I thought he would behave differently with me shows how sick my thinking was.

Gabrielle was barely 6 lbs. and had problems breathing, then she got pneumonia. The doctor told me, "She's a little sick"...like no big deal, but it turned out to be much worse than that because her heart wasn't formed right. Finally they let her go home with me. Everyone thought she was fine.

I went back to Jose's apartment long enough to know that he was just the same, didn't give a shit about us. Every day in the hospital I had gone to the chapel to pray for the strength necessary to do what I had to do. I knew my parents would continue to care for Miranda if I wasn't around and I knew I could not provide what Gabrielle needed. It seemed the solution was to place her for adoption—then kill myself. I was depressed, couldn't eat, couldn't function normally or remember stuff.

When I called my mom, she knew right away I was

in bad trouble, came to get me and the baby. Then she called my counselor, made arrangements to put Gabrielle in foster care while I went to a psycho ward. About three weeks later, I was able to sign papers to give up Gabrielle. My mom went with me. Jose had been harassing us with phone calls, threatening to take the baby himself, get an attorney to fight the adoption, all kinds of ugly stuff.

I was able to choose a couple from letters, but I wasn't offered the chance to meet them. While I don't even know their first names, they know mine because Gabrielle had so many medical records before she was even six months old that someone forgot to remove names along the line. It seems like it's out of balance to me because I would bet they have looked in the phone book for my address and I have sent them photos of me and Miranda.

They know who I am, what I look like, while they only sent me three letters with one picture of Gabrielle alone each time. I don't think they will contact me anymore, which makes me sad. Never would I do anything to interfere with their lives. I know Gabrielle has had major surgery and I'm so grateful she has a family who can support and love her. I hope that some day she will understand my decision.

LESLIE

"My family wants me to act like my baby is dead. They expect me to pick up and keep going...they have no idea how I feel."

Attending AA meetings several times a week, Leslie struggles with her addiction to alcohol and drugs. She is a bright, verbal 24-year-old who explains that she never felt she truly belonged in her own family. Leslie sees herself as being different physically—i.e. large-boned versus petite like her half-sisters—and she is deeply hurt by her biological father's refusal to acknowledge her as a daughter.

Able to remain sober and drug free through her pregnancy, Leslie's life has been in turmoil since she gave birth to Cameron, who was placed with a family who agreed to an open adoption. Shortly after, Leslie was astonished to learn that her own mother had had her first child at age 15, over 30 years ago, and that he had been placed for adoption too. Her mother's wish to see Cameron at the hospital and her joy at meeting his adoptive parents took on new meaning for Leslie.

ঔ

From the outside, my family looks like it has everything—a big house, cars—even a beachfront view—and my stepfather is an successful businessman in our town. Everyone respects our family. My stepfather built his life out of nothing. He was an abused child—beat very badly by his stepdad—and there were a lot of kids in the family, so his ideal view of what a family should be was related totally to money. If you could buy what was needed, then everything was O.K. My stepdad, however, was never emotionally involved with us—at least, that's how I feel.

My own father is someone I have never met, though I know who he is. Basically, he has totally rejected my existence. Once I tried to see him, when I was 13 and was told at the door to get lost. I am my mother's second child, she was not married when she became pregnant with me. I know she thought seriously about adoption for me, then did not go through with it. When she married my stepdad, I was still a baby and they had three more children who never knew what it was like to be rejected by their father like I was.

My mother has been the only person always there for me, but my brother and sisters can't understand that. They have each other—in addition to our mother and my stepfather. Though I never thought of myself as having a father, I had lots of things! A new bike every year, a car at age 16. I was spoiled rotten that way. My approach to dealing with my family has been to get high. Our house was a place where, if you wanted to see dad, you practically had to make an appointment. When he came home angry or drunk, everybody disappeared. I would go to my room. The older kids got in their cars, I went to my room.

My first encounter with alcohol was when I was 10 years old at a birthday party. There was a beer tent set up and everybody kept asking me to bring them a drink. Back and forth, I ran, tasting each one until I was totally bombed. My mother doesn't drink at all, she's scared to death of it because of how other people's drinking has affected her life, but the bar in our house has always held every alcoholic beverage imaginable, so I had lots of opportunity to get whatever I wanted!

At age 12, my grandfather died. He had been a big resource for me. I loved going to his house, playing cards and he was a big animal lover too—like me. It was more fun at his place than my home. When he died, that's when Leslie went away. When we came back from the funeral home for the wake, everyone was laughing and joking while I was a nut case. I asked one of the adults why no one was crying? Why was I the only one? He handed me a beer and that's how I learned at a real young age that I didn't need to feel things. A beer could fix that!

When mom and my stepdad fought, I turned to alcohol. Up in my room. With my drink, that's how I dealt with it. I never went out anywhere. By my teens, I was a closet drinker! All during eighth grade, I would leave for school, walking right past my principal's house—then go into the woods and drink. Sometimes I took my cat with me, walked down a back trail—then just sat and got bombed. Well, the principal tracked my movements, actually wrote down dates and then he told my parents. To keep it out of the court system and out of public knowledge, my parents decided to send me to boarding school.

It cost them $50,000 to send me to this uppity school. Everybody could think, "wow," and be impressed, but it was just one way my family uses money to keep things out of public knowledge. My first week in school, I didn't have to do the usual bullshit that new students went through. This was, by the way, a military school with a ratio of 1 girl to 30 guys! I really felt uprooted. At 13, I didn't understand really why I had to be away from home and I felt very alone.

My mom visited me about once a month, my stepdad, once a year. The school was very hard academically. My parents adored the idea that a person had to have a high I.Q. to get into the place! The officers who dealt with me on an everyday basis eventually got the idea that I was using alcohol. My tack officer kept hammering at me to go to AA. She wanted me to stay in school because they could sort of control me; you know, it was a 24-hour thing. I was at least in the barracks and locked up every night at 11:00 P.M.

I got chummy finally with some older students who were in the band like me. When you hang out with upperclassmen, you learn fast. My best friend was from New York City and when I went there with her, I got introduced to drugs. How I love getting high! I don't have to deal with anything, not life in general, not my emotions. Pot and opium, which you know, is not a drug to mess with. Finally, I got busted for drugs, expelled from school. My parents went white.

Back to public school I went until I got kicked out of there too. A couple of times, I was in a rehab center, then a psychiatric institution 'cause when I got mad, I'd get violent, hitting walls. Certain things would set me off like wanting to know why my biological father rejected me. Once everyone led me to believe that he was coming to talk to me in the hospital, but he didn't show up. I blamed my mother then. Everyone in the family knew *both* their biological parents except me. No one would talk about my biological father to me. Instead I was supposed to be attached to my stepdad. When he decided to adopt me, I didn't have a clue to what was going on. In first grade, a pair of lawyers came to my school, asking me questions.

"Do you love your stepdad?" What was I supposed to say? No? It scared the hell out of me, having guys in three-piece suits in front of me. If I could do it over again, I would not agree to being adopted because there was no emotion between us. My family's biggest concern is their image rather than feelings.

"What happens here stays here." Every night I heard that speech. When my stepdad pulled in the driveway, we tried to gauge his mood for the evening. If he had a decent day, dinner would be normal. Nine times out of 10, something would be wrong and he'd get drunk. We all had to be home for dinner—no matter what—or he'd go looking for us. Our house revolved around his moods.

My brother was also on drugs. Alcohol and drugs were our way out. To me, there was no other way to deal with things. My sex life began when I was 11. An older cousin raped me. For my age, I was big, looked older. He was in his 20s. After that sex meant nothing to me. I tried to kill myself too. Not only did I end up in a straitjacket, I was in a full body suit! The clincher, probably, was being in jail. Hearing those doors slam was not something I liked! At 19 I decided to try to get myself straight. Since I'd been in a mental institution, I was able to get disability checks every month, so I decided to get some technical training far away from my family. They promised to help me financially too if I'd stay off drugs and alcohol.

I moved as far away as I could get, trying to function on my own. My psychiatrist felt I should be away from the family games, then I could realize the difference between who I am and who everyone in my family is. Once I had an apartment, I started school and attended regular AA meetings. That's where I met Gordy. He was 20 years older than me—married and had his own business. Soon I was working for him, paying my own bills and not needing money from my mom. He was so nice to me. I knew he was having problems with his marriage. In fact, once we started going together, I thought his marriage was over.

Long before we had sex together, we became friends, which for me was weird. My other relationships with guys were centered about sex or drugs. Gordy and I *talked*; it was something totally different. For a while we were the big AA couple, but looking back now I can see I wasn't staying sober for myself. I wasn't doing anything for Leslie. At the table, I said the right words, but I was playing an old game. Gordy knew just what buttons to press with me. About the time I realized I was pregnant, I also figured out Gordy was trying to reconcile with his wife, had really been faithful to no one.

Suddenly, Gordy was never available. I did all the phone calling, but he could never talk. When I told him I was pregnant, he wanted me to get an abortion and I was seriously thinking about that. My classes at school kept me occupied and I didn't want to mess that up. My grade point average was one of the best and my parents were sort of thinking I was doing O.K.—not the big fuck-up!

From day one, I told Gordy, "It's either an abortion or adoption. I'm not going to raise a baby." With my background, I knew I wasn't ready to be a mother. I couldn't take care of myself—a baby would have nothing with me! In fact, I'm not big on kids at all. Gordy couldn't get $300 together without his wife knowing—for an abortion— and I finally realized that I had to do something by myself because the pregnancy was getting obvious. Things fell into place after that. I went to a private agency and told my mom. She was flabbergasted. This would be her first grandchild and she kept asking, "Who?"

My mom was very worried about me being so far away, alone and pregnant. I told her my relationship with the baby's father was over and I tried to handle everything without causing problems. I stayed in school, stayed off drugs and alcohol, which was easier, doing it for the baby's sake. Once Gordy came over and had everything set for a good time—joints rolled and ready, my favorite booze. It was so tempting...but I said "No." I could see he was a real con and pulled away from him.

It was hard because I really cared for Gordy. Part of me still does, but there was no life for me with him. A good time is all he wants—even when he's throwing AA program talk around. This is a man who's gonna go off the deep end someday. I believe that, all the things he's into—like faking a break-in to his own home and then collecting insurance on a supposedly stolen stereo system and VCR. He's real big on guns too—has a whole collection that he loves to sit around with, look at...shoot once in a while. When the cops come into the neighborhood, he acts like the concerned citizen. A big game for him!

At first my mom kept the pregnancy secret from everyone else in the family. Slowly, everyone found out. My stepdad was the last to know and that wasn't until after Cameron was born and everything was a done deal. His only comment was, "How are you?" "Fine, Dad." He has no idea of what is going on around him.

Phone calls were flying back and forth all over the country about screw-up Leslie. They all thought adoption was best, flat out told me there was no way this baby would be accepted by our family. My mom was the most understanding, the one who would listen to me. Right off, she planned to fly out to be there for my labor.

In my eighth month, I chose a family, met with them. They were the perfect couple, willing to be totally open. I could hardly believe they were real! Jeff and Gail were a big part of helping it all go smoothly for me. When I had false labor, they spent hours in the hospital and we got to know each other really well. At first, I wanted to have the baby, then have no more contact with them, but after delivery, I knew I had to have more. All these feelings came up. I wanted them to hold him, care for him from the very beginning. Never did they seem to be afraid that I would change my mind. They were so relaxed, laid back—yet happy too.

My mom came with all kinds of presents. She

asked if she could see Cameron, hold him, and I said, "Of course! You can meet Jeff and Gail too." If it had been a closed adoption, I never could have done it. I would have walked out of that hospital with Cameron, knowing I would not be a good parent for him. Instead it was very reassuring to see Gail hold him, see how he fit in with them perfectly and to know they weren't going to shut me out. I trust them 100 percent and I know exactly what Cameron will have with them...everything I can't give him.

When I explained the open concept to my family, they freaked out. Except mom. One of my sisters said, "What the hell is mom doing there? What are you going to do—run around with all kinds of pictures of the baby? Are they all going to come visit us, maybe stay with Mom and Dad?"

They didn't even try to understand how I felt or want to be a part of welcoming my child. It blows me away that they can't rise above their petty little worries, their perfect lives. Because I gave up Cameron, I'm not supposed to feel anything for him! My sister came right out with, "He means nothing to us!"

My family doesn't know that I saw Gail, Jeff and Cameron several times over the first few months, that I bought him a christening outfit and was invited to attend. I'm not going to deny that I had a baby and that he's getting the best life possible with his adoptive parents. As shaky as I am, I still know I made the right decision for Cameron.

I finished my semester in school and then Gordy came back into my life. His wife had filed for divorce. Now, things flip-flopped. He was calling me constantly, wanting us to be together, wanting to know how Cameron is doing. There is no way I'm going to share the openness I have with Jeff and Gail with Gordy. He wasn't there for me at all during the pregnancy, but at the same time, he's the only person who understands. Gordy was bugging me all the time, I couldn't handle it.

I started using again—alcohol, any drug I could get hold of—and that scares me. The stakes are higher now. Getting high has been my life for so long, I don't know any other way. I can't stay clean just for me, I can't have any kind of life with Gordy either. And I sure don't want Cameron knowing someday that he has an addict for a birthmother. I decided it'd be best if I left the area—start over somewhere.

My biggest fear is that Cameron will feel rejected someday—by his birthfather or by me. I don't want that to happen. My biological father not wanting me, not being willing to send me a picture or acknowledge my existence is the worst possible thing to feel. I'm not a heartless person. I know my son is cared for and with my addiction, I don't know what I'm going to do from one day to the next. That's the bottom line—I am so fucked up. With the adoption decision, I am comfortable and confident. With me—Leslie—the way my life has been, it would have been better if my mother had done what my biological father wanted: get an abortion.

I wish my mom would have gone through with an abortion. I'd rather I had not been born at all.

BRIGITTE

"Their attitude toward her changed, I believe, after the birth of their own child. Then she became second-hand."

Exhausted by her efforts to support and care for two toddler daughters in 1978, Brigitte trusted a relative to take over while she was hospitalized with an illness. Temporary care extended to several months—then—plans for private placement with two separate families were initiated and arranged by the relative. Feeling she could not provide all she wanted her daughters to have, Brigitte signed consents to adoption.

A high school dropout who had married at age 16 to avoid an unhappy situation with her alcoholic parents, Brigitte struggled with feelings of low self-esteem and failure. Her husband, two years older than she, had abused her physically and emotionally, providing no support for his daughters after their divorce. Once her little girls were gone, Brigitte never expected to see either one again. From an emotional low that included a period of drinking, Brigitte gradually improved her working skills and personal relationships.

By the time she was 30 years old, Brigitte was in her second marriage, "a good one this time," and was the parent of two more children. She was astonished to receive a phone call in 1992 from the adoptive parents of her youngest daughter, who was now 15 years old and committed to a state institution. The family offered to relinquish *their* rights, giving custody to Brigitte and her husband.

Growing up, I was the second oldest of five girls. My parents never seemed to get along together. Dad was a bully while my mom withdrew from everyone, going about chores like cleaning the house or cooking the meals—then curling up in a chair with a book, shutting everything out. On the outside they appeared to be a normal middle class family; on the inside, it was kind of a nightmare. I was 10 years old when the last girl was born and when she was two months old, my mother packed her bags and left us for good. She couldn't take any of us anymore, went to her own parents.

While I can't say everything was Dad's fault, he was a difficult person to live with. Both were drinkers, though mom quit after she left. All we heard was how she was a no-good person. Eventually none of us mentioned her to Dad 'cause he would go off on a tirade. Neither one was what I would describe as warm or affectionate. Dad hired a housekeeper, but once we came home from school, my oldest sister and I babysat the others. I was never allowed to go anywhere else after school.

In my teens I began to rebel. When I wanted to go out on Saturday evenings, Dad would yell, "No, you have to take care of your sisters!" I began to lie, saying I was going to the library, instead hanging out on a corner with my friends. At 15, it was just something we did and I had to get out of that house. Dad caught on, told me I was a bad influence on my sisters. I was smoking and my grades were slipping too. One day I came home from school and saw all my belongings in boxes on the back porch.

"You're out of here," Dad told me. I called my mother who lived in another town and went to live with her for about a year. Looking back, I think I was probably a depressed teenager because I had trouble concentrating. Even though I went to school every day, I couldn't keep track of my locker combination or what class I was suppose to be in. It wasn't that I deliberately ignored my school work, I just couldn't focus. My mother was drinking again. All I ever heard, it seemed, from anyone was how bad I was. When I dropped out of school at age 16, then it was, "See I told you how bad she was!"

Though I had no friends, I met a guy, Sam, who didn't like his parents either and we decided to get married as soon as he turned 18. His parents were much older and very strict, very domineering though; they also believed their baby son could do no wrong. His dad found a job for him and I told my parents I was pregnant, which was not true, so they would give their permission for me to marry. Both of us wanted an escape, some place else to be.

Sam and I got a small apartment and six months later, I was really pregnant. He went to work every day, came home and began to slap me for the stupidest things—like burning his pork chops. Small stuff like that. I was shocked but blamed myself, tried harder and began the pattern of thinking it was somehow my fault because no person would hit another without a good reason. When Nicole was born in 1973, our financial problems began and the beatings became more severe. Sam only worked part-time—then I was pregnant again and Nina was born, 15 months after Nicole.

One evening I was invited to a wedding reception with my mother and a friend. It lasted longer than I thought and I was afraid to go home, knowing Sam would be furious, so I told my mom about the beatings. She went back to the apartment with me to get the babies and to pack. At least she stood up for me. All I can say good about Sam was that at least he never hit the babies. After a couple of days at my mom's, she told me, "I don't make enough money to support all three of you. I've talked to your dad and he says you can live with him."

It was like going out of the frying pan into the fire, but I had no choice with two small babies, no job...For six months I tried it and was never able to do anything right. "Why are you wearing that?" or "Why are you eating that?" My dad was constantly on my case. Sam had gone back to his parents, had no interest in his children, while our apartment stood empty. I decided to try to make it on my own. I moved back into the apartment and looked for a job. With no training, no high school diploma, there was nothing but waitressing for me and there was very little money in that. Then I had to worry about babysitters.

Sam started coming over, wanted us to work it out together. Since I was sinking fast all alone, I agreed to try again. That was a mistake. We were barely surviving financially—the electricity was shut off and Sam was seeing other women. The beatings began again, I had cuts and bruises all the time. There was no great love between us. There wasn't even survival. To me it was rock bottom. I packed up our things again and went to my dad's. It was the only place I had to go.

By then my oldest sister was married and my dad had placed my younger sisters in a children's home. He blamed me for that, forgetting *he* was the one who threw my belongings on the porch when I was 15 years old! According to him, if I hadn't "left home," hadn't been so bad, *I* would have been there to help with the other girls. Consequently, my sisters and I have never been really close, though we exchange letters and on some weekends I would visit them at the home.

Six nights a week I waitressed, getting home at 3:00 A.M., sleeping till 7:00, getting up with Nicole and Nina and starting all over. After a few months, Dad announced, "It's ridiculous to have you here with your two kids while my daughters are in a home. I'm getting them out and you can leave!" During this time I wasn't receiving any child support—lawyers were chasing Sam around. My job paid $253 twice a month.

I had to find an apartment and move out. No matter how hard I tried, it seemed I couldn't do anything right. When I applied for food stamps, they said I made too much, even though they counted the child support I wasn't getting!

I was very down on myself—like: "Other people can manage, why can't you?" I couldn't figure out what was wrong with me! I tried having a roommate who could help with the rent. I still had to pay for babysitters—and for a while, that worked. Then she moved out. I tried holding two jobs, bartending...tried getting a cheaper apartment and for a little while, I could manage, keeping the girls fed and a roof over our heads, but bit by bit, I fell behind. When I lost my car, I had to find a different job in walking distance. There I was in two cheap rooms with a bath and a two-year-old and a three-year-old, but I could walk to work and to the grocery store. Everything under control until I got sick and was taken to the hospital. I called my oldest sister, asked her to get the kids from the sitter's and she said O.K. Then she comes to the hospital and volunteers to care for Nicole and Nina until I get well. Of course, at that point, I was grateful.

A couple of days later, she and her husband come to the hospital with a proposal. "Things are not going well for you," they pointed out, "why don't you let us care for the girls until you're really back on your feet?" I knew I was not doing right by Nicole and Nina, barely getting through each day so I agreed. When they suggested legal guardianship for a year, I felt it would be best. Once I was well, I'd visit the kids, take them places, but I wasn't doing much better workwise. Beat down was how I felt, tending bar at nights and sleeping in the day.

It was close to a year before I was able to find a bartender's position in a better class of place—and a nice little apartment and a used car. I lined up a baby sitter for the kids too. Going to my sister's home, I told her I was ready to resume care of my children and she said *no*! "We don't think it's right that you take them, working nights like you do, serving alcohol and your neighborhood is not that good either." They refused to give me my girls.

From there, I gave up—after trying so hard, it seemed nothing was going to be any better for me—why try? It was useless. I began drinking, working just enough to get by and, after six months had gone by, my sister announced to me, "You're never going to pull yourself together and I can't keep these kids forever. Why not let someone adopt them? I've already talked to a couple who wants Nina."

There was more discussion—finally, feeling I couldn't handle anything, I agreed and Nina at age three went to a family. My sister and their attorney were the go-betweens. A month later they found a couple who wanted to take Nicole. Sam and I were divorced by then and he was happy to sign his rights as a parent away because it relieved him of paying child support, having his wages garnisheed.

While I didn't see myself as having a drinking problem, I couldn't stand to be home alone so I would go out with friends to a bar—or dancing. Everyone else would be ready to go home by midnight—not me, I'd want to stay. A man I dated off and on, Charles, knew about my children being placed for adoption, expressed an opinion to me that he didn't like the idea, but he felt I had to do what I had to do. Over the next year, Charles and I became closer.

My life slowly got better. Finding a job in an office helped me realize I wasn't a stupid person because I passed all their tests with flying colors. Two years later, Charles and I got married. The only person in my family who would speak to me was my mother. The rest couldn't understand how I could let my girls go, passing judgment on me. Charles' mother was sympathetic. Once she said to me, "It must have been awful for you."

Charles and I had a son and daughter, two years apart. His job took us to another state. Our marriage was good; we have always been happy together. I never thought I would see Nina or Nicole again. Over 10 years passed. I had a home, a family and self-esteem. Out of the blue I was contacted by a distant relative who had information about Nina—she said Nina's adoptive parents wanted to talk to me by phone and I agreed. Her father told me that since entering her teens, Nina was rebelling and had gotten herself into some nasty situations. The bottom line was that they didn't want her anymore.

Needless to say, I was shocked. It was like I was being told, "Look at the mess you gave us. What are you going to do about it?" Nina was into drugs, alcohol and had run away from them several times, eventually landing in a psychiatric hospital. The counselors there said she had unresolved issues with her birthmother... so—Nina's adoptive parents decided she could not come back into their house! She was 15 years old!

It was a very confusing time, but I didn't hesitate. "Sure, I'll take her back," I told them. She was—to me—absolutely—still my daughter. I could not have said no anymore than I could fly. He gave me the name of the institution Nina was in and said they would relinquish their legal rights. I flew out west to visit her. Nina had no real memory of her first three years with me and was pretty angry with her adoptive family. She felt the early years of her life had been fine—until her parents had a biological daughter when Nina was 12 years old.

Basically, Nina's counselors agreed that she had been rejected by her adoptive family long before she rejected them. She had also been told what a terrible mother I had been to her and she believed it until we got to know each other better. We had a lot of conversations, crying and yelling as I tried to help her understand that I had always loved her, that I had placed her because I loved her and wanted her to be cared for properly. It was not a decision made without emotion.

It took six months before Nina was released to me and Charles. He was very supportive as we all adjusted in our home. Certainly, it wasn't 100 percent easy for any one of us, but I think Nina understands better now what happened. She likes her little brother a lot; is more cool with her sister, who lost her place as the oldest child in our household. They manage to converse at dinner and then go in opposite directions. I think Nina resents that her sister has been with me since day one. She blames herself for her behavior, thinking she caused her rejection by the adoptive parents.

I don't want to say anything negative about adoption in general—it just didn't happen to work out in this particular instance. As far as I know, everything is fine with Nicole. Maybe someday she'll search for me, she's over 18 by now. I won't initiate a search because I made an agreement and I feel bound to live by it.

HILARY

"When Jamie's adoptive parents invited me over for a visit, it was really nice. I mean they invited me—I didn't ask."

It is the exception, rather than the rule, that a pregnant teenager will have her boyfriend's support emotionally throughout her pregnancy. Even less often does the boy participate in counseling. Hilary and Jon were committed together to carrying out their adoption plan for their son, Jamie, born while they were still in high school.

Barely five feet tall and less than 100 lbs., Hilary's solemn demeanor arouses concern for her well being. Jon was her emotional lifeline for two years and their separation, subsequent break-up left Hilary to fend for herself. She speaks in a flat monotone, the strength of her words not matching her fragile, subdued appearance.

❧

If I could give advice to a pregnant teenager, I'd tell her, "Take care of yourself. Don't be afraid to ask for help because you need someone to talk to and don't let your emotions rule. Do what is best for your baby, not what you want."

If my baby's adoption were not open, I don't think I could have handed him over to a stranger. The idea of abuse is very scary. More advice I would give is that a girl should meet the couple, get to know their temperament and whether they can be trusted, not only now but later too. The willingness to be open was what I liked about Gary and Debra plus they were so nice. I saw how they were raising their daughter too, how close they were and I wanted that for Jamie. I used to wish for a family just like them.

My parents were divorced when I was five years old. Being scared when they were yelling at each other is about all I remember. They were too young to be parents, to be married. My dad was still in high school when my mom became pregnant with me—that's the reason they married. It was hard for them. Knowing that, I didn't want the same thing to happen again, Jamie's dad staying with me because of a pregnancy. After my parent's divorce, I grew up back and forth between them. When my dad moved to California, I lived with him over a year because my mom had a boyfriend I didn't get along with at all.

Both of my parents are smart, should have gone to college. In fact, mom was a straight-A student. Now she works in a store and is very insecure, keeps falling for guys who are not good for her. The man who lives with her doesn't work, uses drugs and always called me names. I tried to stay away as much as possible. My dad married again. Sometimes I got along pretty good with my stepmom, but when they began to have problems, it wasn't real pleasant for me either. It's like she was jealous of me and nothing I said was ever right.

I'm the type of person who likes to think for myself. When my dad pushes me to get good grades, it doesn't work, but on my own, if I'm left alone, I can be an excellent student. When I was a sophomore, I began to date. I had a few boyfriends who were no big deal—then I met Jon, my first major love. He was a junior. We had some classes together and lunch hour...Jon is very sensitive though he tries to look tough. For about six months, we were just friends, then we became sexually active. Actually, I was the last one in my group of friends to have sex; they were beginning to make me feel weird.

Jon was very open about being adopted himself. That surprised me, but when I became pregnant, it was probably the reason he wanted adoption for our baby.

I tried to protect myself from a pregnancy, went to Planned Parenthood and got birth control pills, but when I ran out, I couldn't afford any more. Jon refused to use a condom, said he didn't like them. In his senior year, right at the beginning of the school year, I knew I was pregnant. The very first month, I felt different and told Jon right away.

"Are you sure?" was his response. I didn't want Jon to stay with me just because of the pregnancy and thought briefly about abortion. Knowing I couldn't go through with that, adoption was the only answer. If we were through with school, things would have been different...as it was, we needed to go to school. Jon worked a lot of hours, weekends and evenings, delivering pizza. Most of my money came from him, I should say all because neither of my parents gave me an allowance. Home, with my mom, was scary because of her boyfriend and by then my dad was living in Texas.

Going to school, being pregnant was enough. I knew I couldn't work a job too. I thought a lot: I wanted our baby to have things I didn't have, to have an opportunity for a good education some day. There was no way Jon and I could do that for him. My mom found out by reading my mail when the first bill from the doctor's came.

"What's this?" was all she said. Then she wanted me to get an abortion—only it wasn't her choice. We never talked about it again though later on Mom did buy me some maternity clothes.

Jon went with me to the same agency where he had been adopted. Because I was scared to live at home, afraid my mom's boyfriend would do something to hurt me or the baby, my caseworker suggested a foster home. That was the best time for me. The couple was very nice and it was peaceful. Nobody bugged me or called me names. I didn't know there were places like that out there—for teens who need help.

My caseworker told me about open adoption and I knew that was the way it had to be. Three times during my pregnancy, Jon and I met with Debra and Gary, who are in their 40s and have one biological daughter, Melissa. She is 12, actually taller than I am. We went out to dinner with them. I knew they were the kind of people who would keep their promises.

Jamie was born the week of my final exams in school. The worse day was leaving the hospital and signing the papers. After I finished my exams, I went to live with my dad. Leaving Jon was not what I really wanted to do, but there was no way I could go to Mom's. We planned that I would complete my senior year, then Jon and I could be together because by then he would be working full-time—get an apartment and maybe go to college.

It didn't work out that way.

My dad and stepmother lived out in the middle of nowhere and my new school was small, not at all what I was used to. Everyone knew everyone else. I made some friends, but my stepmother was busy telling everyone my life story, while my dad pressed me to do better in school and tried to be strict with me, wouldn't let me drive his car or provide any money for things I needed. I started selling my clothes in order to buy make-up, shoes, stuff like that. Any little thing done on my behalf, nobody let me forget it, rubbing it in so I had to say "thank you" a thousand times.

Still—life wasn't too bad. Mid-year, Jon wanted me to move back and live with him, but I was afraid to do it in the middle of my senior year. I couldn't tell him, "hey, I'm scared," to be dependent on him. After I graduated, it would be easier to find a job, but he took it to mean I didn't want to and stopped calling as much. He didn't ask much about Jamie either, except to want a picture. Debra was sending me a lot, but I told Jon, "You know where they are—ask for yourself."

Jon never called them or saw them again. I wasn't happy about that because I don't ever want Jamie to think his birthparents didn't care. If I were adopted and my birthfather didn't ask about me, I would feel he didn't love me. When I learned Jon had a new girlfriend, I got depressed even though I wanted him to be happy.

I felt so alone, I tried to kill myself. I was really upset, sick—had fooled around with the idea before, but this time I wanted to die. It wasn't about the adoption or missing Jamie. I was glad about that. I believe in God so I thought I'd go to heaven. My family would be real glad that I was gone. After I slit my wrists, I couldn't believe I was really doing it, called a friend who came to my house and took me to the hospital where they stitched me up.

Then I had to talk to a psychiatrist who gave me pills for depression. They made me irritable; after a while I quit taking them. Talking to the psychiatrist felt good and it's supposed to become a family thing with my dad and stepmom. Going back to school was hard because everyone knew, figured I was stupid to try suicide. The school counselors gave me a bunch of tests because now I am labeled "disabled" because of depression. If it helps me get some training—like in computers, that will be okay.

In less than two months, I will graduate and then I plan to move out. Even though my dad wants me to go to college, he refuses to help me financially—in fact, he says when I graduate, I'll have to pay room and board. Without a car, stuck in the country, where am I supposed to find a job?

I may as well be by myself. I want to go back, establish a better relationship with my mom but I don't want to live with her. Can't. Even though Jon is living with a girl, I heard he is unhappy and missed me. He goes to night school now. My goals are: to graduate, find a job and go back for more schooling eventually.

I want to be independent. I'd like to be able to take care of myself.

BETH

"The attraction of having a 19-year-old interested in me when I wasn't even 14 was incredible. It never even occurred to me that I could get pregnant."

In her first year of high school, Beth delivered a son whom she wanted desperately to parent. Without consistent support from her adoptive mother and father, she reluctantly agreed to allow her married sister to adopt her baby. Within two years, Beth, "seeking love through sex," was pregnant again.

Her daughter, Rachelle, was born in 1985. This time the decision to choose adoption came from Beth herself, working through an agency. A high school dropout, involved in alcohol and drugs off and on, Beth was on a downward spiral. An abusive relationship with a man who beat her repeatedly, finally fracturing her skull, was the environment in which she bore her third child at age 22.

"By that time," Beth explains, "I had mother instincts going all through me with no way to let them out. I had no one to help me, but I wanted to be a mom."

Fierce in her desire to construct a life for herself and her third baby, Beth filed charges against the baby's father and entered a federally sponsored work education program. She also launched a search for her own birthparents.

With her quick wit that almost masks her insecurity, Beth appears street-smart. It is only in her diary writing that she reveals her vulnerability and promises herself:

"I won't always be stepped on."

ও

A lot of the problems I had growing up probably would have been the same even if I had not been adopted. Other kids did think I was strange because I was adopted and I remember telling my mom I didn't have to listen to her because she wasn't my real mother. After I saw the look on her face, I never wanted to say that again. I was about nine years old then and for as long as I can remember, I felt like I was standing still, watching life go by—watching other kids laugh and play but never belonging, never feeling part of anything. My parents did their best to help me feel loved and wanted, but I was a confused child.

My parents were already in their 40s and had two teenagers, practically grown, when they brought me into the family at the age of six weeks, so it seemed like I was an only child. Looking back at family pictures, I identified mostly with my father, I think, because I was always wearing jeans and a tee shirt, had short hair too—like a boy. I liked hanging out in my dad's wood shop, hanging upside down from tree branches…by the fourth grade, there were problems at school, mostly academic ones and I was held back a grade. My mom was in the hospital for six months, which I have no real memory of, but my sister became the person in charge of the house.

Maybe I have blocked that time period out. Later I found out my mother had a nervous breakdown, pulled her own hair right out. I didn't have any friends, was lonely and sad. At school I had counselors, but every time I began to feel comfortable, they went away. When I was 11 years old, my father moved out of the house, which at least stopped my feeling torn between my parents. There was no way my mom could control me—she couldn't even drive a car and had never held a job! Things were pretty tough for us as I grew more rebellious.

My dad married again when I was 13—a woman with three kids, one as old as I, and she fought with her mother as much as I did! My stepmom tried to be my mom when I already had one plus my sister! I didn't trust anyone, didn't know how to make myself feel better, but I began to discover I felt something like love through flirting—and then sex. It started after the summer I went to camp where my mom found a job. There were riding lessons (which I loved) and it was great. Then I returned home and met a boy at the mall one day. He was 14—walked me home and that was my first love! He was a virgin too.

No one had ever talked to me about sex. The generation gap in our family was huge. My mom was in her 50s, my sister had her own family. The group I hung out with were 16 or 17-year-olds because at 13 I looked older than I was. They told me about sex and I was petrified! Couldn't really understand how it would fit! All of us kids got together at my boyfriend's garage while his mom worked. There were couches, a TV, stereo and no adult was ever around. The only rule was "no alcohol," which happened once in a while and a lot of the kids smoked pot. After about four months of being friends, while I was in the eighth grade, I had intercourse with my boyfriend.

After a while we broke up. People drifted in and out of our group and some were much older—19, 20 years old. That's how I met Tom. The older kids would have parties—with drinking and I hung out all the time with them. Tom was 19, interested in me who wasn't even in high school yet! It blew my mind away—before long we were going steady, having sex. He knew how to take his time with me. Tom was very affectionate, very patient—he knew what to do and how to do it! When both of our moms found out, they threw fits and I had to break off the relationship. For birth control Tom had used a condom.

I wasn't supposed to see Tom, but I still hung around with his sister, Linda, who invited me to spend the night at her house. I don't remember if a party was planned or if it just happened to come together. Someone handed me a glass of rum and Coke, that's when I started to drink. Everyone else was smoking pot or using other drugs. What I didn't know until several years later was that someone slipped me a hit of LSD. The night was a mess. I remember bits and pieces of it: Tom wanted to have sex, I didn't. We fought, he outweighed me. I remember being in the basement, him throwing me down and feeling like I was losing my mind. The drugs were doing things to me too.

There was a tiny bathroom. I ran in there afterwards, must have been blown out of my mind because I couldn't figure out how to get out of there. Looking in the mirror, I was so scared, I smashed it and when I brought my hands down, I was bleeding. The cuts were tiny, but while I looked at them, my veins came out of my wrists and turned into snakes, coming after me. I broke down the door, ran out of the house and ended up sleeping in a park, inside a concrete tunnel.

That happened in mid-August. In September I started ninth grade, realizing a month later that I was pregnant. When I was almost seven months along, my mom said to me one day, "It's been a while since I bought you anything for your period." Then we talked and the next thing I knew, I was in a doctor's office. My parents flipped out, my dreams were blown away. I felt I had let my parents down. I wondered too about my birthmother and how she might feel.

At school they told me I couldn't come back because I was too far along—I weighed 180 lbs. Maybe they were afraid I'd go into labor and was too young to understand the signs. A week later the school officials changed their minds so I went back. Everyone was nice to me except for the snobby girls who never liked me anyway. Tom's sister, however, was real vicious to me, tried to beat me up. Suddenly we were major enemies and everyone else was afraid of her. Actually Linda was the meanest bitch in the school.

I think I had been friends with her just to avoid being her enemy. Now she was after me. One day I was walking home from school, a car pulled over and out jumps Linda yelling, "I'm gonna give you a homemade abortion."

"Sure you are!" I'm screaming back and I'm bigger all the way around than she is! We ended up on the ground; she hit me in the head and kept trying to punch my stomach. I saw red then and pounded her, just pounded her into the ground. From that point, I was the baddest bitch in the school: I had to learn to fight right there.

Tom came to me and said he wanted to get married and take care of me and the baby. He enlisted in the Marines and became even a bigger drunk than he was. By then, I had no interest in him—had met a boy named Karl who was the first guy I *really* loved. Even though I was pregnant, we did everything together like roller-skating. Karl was 16 and had his own car. He was good to me, treated me like it was his own baby I was carrying. His parents were both alcoholics—never abusive—just drank all the time.

My parents were trying to talk me into adoption. I refused, not wanting my kid to go through what I did—always wondering about my background, never knowing. That's the worse thing about being adopted. So I decided to give a shot at being a parent. My mom said I couldn't live at home; Karl said I could live with his parents and when my son, Joey, was born, Karl was supposed to take me home from the hospital. Instead my sister showed up and took everything over. She wouldn't let either of us get in Karl's car. I was tired and wanted to be left alone. I wanted to try to work everything out so I could raise Joey with Karl helping, so I went to live with my sister not making a fuss.

Joey was the only blood relative I had. I took him

every place I went, I breast fed him and Karl would pick us up, take us to the doctors or to visit his parents. They adored Joey too. I was 14 years old, didn't know the first thing about raising a baby. I had never followed any rules or regulations and to top it off, I think I went through post-partum depression. My mom helped out some for the first six weeks, then she said she had enough, that she wasn't going to do this any longer. It wasn't like I was asking her to raise my baby—I just needed some assistance.

I planned to go back to school and try to get welfare but it seemed my mother and sister sabotaged me every way they could. Finally, my sister kicked me out of the house. I went to my dad's. They wouldn't let me be a parent there. Every time Joey cried, someone picked him up until I had a baby who wanted to be held non-stop while I had all these chores to do around the house. I'd put him in a playpen—someone would do something else. I got fed up. One morning when I woke up I saw Joey's eyes were swollen, blood coming out of one. I panicked, called Karl and we took Joey to the hospital. He'd had a reaction to drops in his eyes and when they gave him some medication, everything was fine.

My mom, I know, was thinking I could not care for Joey properly. She felt everybody else was caring for him. I was under a lot of stress. When she suggested I take a little vacation—rest, visit my older brother and his wife in New York, it sounded wonderful to me. My sister volunteered to care for Joey for two weeks while I was gone. Stupidly, I was happy, never dreaming that they were going to use that vacation as proof of me abandoning my son. My great vacation turned out to be a free babysitting service for my brother. When I got back, Mom and my sister would not let me see Joey.

I got hysterical, I wanted my son. My sister was 30 years old and could do anything she wanted, but the police said there was nothing they could do to help me. I was nothing but a dumb 14-year-old with no right to my own child. No one treated me with any respect; even when I agreed to go to family counseling, it was like I didn't exist. There was no consideration for my feelings. Wanting what was best for Joey, I still had the right, I thought, to try to make a go with him myself or decide what was better for him.

Staying out at Karl's parents' house, I remember sitting in the bay window of the living room, crying. Without his parents, I don't know how I would have made it. I was so angry with my family! The counselor acted like my anger wasn't important, like I didn't have the right to my own feelings. A month passed with us all going to therapy. That counselor was a man who sided 100 percent with my family. He had no idea of what I had gone through carrying Joey and trying to raise him or what it's like to be adopted. All he understood was that I wanted Joey back and he didn't agree.

One day after I had returned to my mom's house to live, I was watching TV while she was at work. That's all I did all day—watch TV in my room and talk to no one. No school. No job. I was a mess, but I think if someone had really tried to understand how I felt, given me some consideration, I would have been able to respond intelligently instead of being so angry and upset. Suddenly into the house come my sister and the counselor, carrying Joey who was now about three months old. They put Joey on the floor on top of a blanket, put a diaper bag beside him and left—like they were saying, "Here you are. Take over."

Then my mom comes home and announces, "You can't live here anymore." It was the same shit all over again with me and Joey ending up back at Karl's house.

The only other person who tried to help me parent was a social worker at an adoption agency. I could talk to her and she listened. She helped me work through how I felt about being adopted.

For almost six months, I had Joey. I finally made arrangements to live with an older girlfriend in exchange for babysitting her kids. We got along great. Then everything fell apart when Joey got sick. His fever went to 105, I took him to the emergency room and he had a bad infection. It got worse. Over the next three days, I just lost it, feeling I couldn't care for him properly. With no one to help me, it was true, I couldn't do it alone. I gave up. I called my sister from the hospital, said she could come get Joey, that I wasn't able to care for him.

Because it was my sister and her husband's wish, I didn't see Joey again for almost two years. By then they had adopted him legally. During that time, I didn't care what happened to me. If I would have had the guts to do so, I would have killed myself. Instead I ran non-stop, from one place to another, sometimes Karl's place or a girlfriend's. I was drinking heavily, sleeping with Karl on and off though our relationship was no longer boyfriend/girlfriend. He was still going to high school—17-years-old while I was living out in the country on a horse farm. Well, I ended up pregnant again—by Karl!

My friends said something about abortion, but there was no way I could do that. I would never condemn anybody for doing that, but it was not a consideration for me, not when I was 14 and pregnant, not when I was 17 and pregnant! Karl had been there for me when I was fighting to keep Joey, but when I was carrying his child, it was another matter. He didn't know how to handle it—again we were both too young. This time I knew I couldn't make it. I didn't know anything about welfare, was a high school drop-out with no place to live and after what I had already put my parents through, I couldn't imagine what they would say.

I told Karl, "I think I'm going to put the baby up for adoption. I'm not sure but I'm thinking about it." Then I told my mom and I went to see the social worker who helped me before. She arranged for me to live at a home in another city. The pregnancy was terrible. From day one until delivery, I was sick. Probably it was emotional, I was depressed and lonely. My mom tried to be kind, tried to understand me as best she could, but there was an enormous generation gap and I had been behaving like a maniac for years.

Karl's parents didn't know what to say or do. By the time I went to the home, I had pretty much made up my mind for adoption. It was a terrible winter, the weather was bad, so I didn't have many visitors. The home had two-bedroom apartments and I had my own. At 17, I was the oldest girl there. Everyone got on my nerves, except for a black girl who became my friend. We had some good times, doing craft work, but I spent a lot of time alone. I didn't want to get attached to anyone. Certainly, I didn't want to get attached to the baby.

At the hospital, we were treated like trash so I told my social worker I wanted to go back to my hometown and deliver there. I didn't want a bunch of nurses or a bunch of counselors buzzing in my ear. I wanted to make my decision on my own. When my daughter was born, I didn't want to get attached to her, knowing what I had to do, but for three days I had her with me in the hospital. I took a million pictures. My parents came to see her. I named her Rachelle after my mom (Rachel) and my sister (Michele). Whenever I thought about keeping her, I shut the thought down and being adopted myself, I think choosing adoption hurt more. I had already lost Joey. Now the second only blood relative I had would not be with me either.

My social worker helped me a lot, really made sure I was O.K. with the adoption decision. I told her I didn't want Rachelle in foster care more than absolutely necessary, definitely not more than two days. I wanted pictures of her for six months and I wanted to give her a white teddy bear. Actually, I would have liked information about her and the family—and photos longer but I was afraid to ask for more and it wasn't offered. It seemed like I never got anything much that I wanted, so I warned myself, "Beth, don't be greedy."

An open adoption would have been 100 percent better. All I know about the family is their religion, that they too like animals, live in the country and that money is not a problem. At six months, I received Rachelle's photos, four of them. She looked just like Karl, blond and blue-eyed and her name had been changed. I tried to imagine what her room looks like. When I saw the photos, I sort of flipped because she looked so different from what she had at birth. Then, her hair was dark and she looked like me.

It is really important to me that Rachelle's family understand that if she ever wants to know me that they help her arrange a meeting. I don't want her to go through the problems I had in dealing with being adopted, people thinking adoptees are different somehow. In school I hated the making of family trees. I couldn't use my parents' background—they weren't mine—even though they were my family. My father told me he didn't even want to tell me I was adopted, he just wanted me to be *his* little girl, no one else's. Well—at 25 years old, I'm still dealing with adoption.

I think I can understand why my birthmother chose adoption for me. She wanted to give me a better life. Whether or not it was, I don't know. Someday I will find my birthparents. I need to know who I look like, what my nationality is, my medical history and whether or not I have brothers and sisters. My parents told me I was Greek. My hair is dark, my skin olive and I've always accepted that. Since I've started searching, I've learned no one knows what my ethnic background is—the doctor just *guessed*! I don't want someone's guess!

Joey is 11 years old now. My relationship with my sister is better and I've always been "Aunt Beth" to him, having to keep my mouth shut all these years at every family gathering. He knows he's adopted and that I was too. At the age of five, he told me that the two of us looked different, not like anyone else in the family, and that is true. Recently my sister told him I was his birthmother. Joey was thrilled. He came running out of the house, down to my car, yelling, "I know. I know."

"What do you know?" I was flabbergasted. No one had warned me. When Joey said, "You're my biological mom!" I thought I would die right there.

He went on. "I've always known. I knew you were the one I came out of…it is so cool, we look alike!"

Now Joey doesn't know what to call me, calls my sister "Aunt Mom." Actually she had done a great job raising him and I told Joey, "I had you; you have my genes, but *she* is your mother. A mom is someone who cares for you, raises you, loves you and is always there." I won't ever let him play us off against each other.

Everyone thinks I have a hard exterior because I hide my feelings. Watching Joey and helping him sort out his adoption helps me understand myself better too. I hope someday Rachelle will know my part of her background. If she wants it, I think she has the right!